TExES Mathematics 7–12 (235) Practice Test Kit
TEACHER CERTIFICATION EXAM

By: Sharon Wynne, M.S.

XAMonline, INC.
Boston

Copyright © 2014 XAMonline, Inc.

All rights reserved. No part of the material protected by this copyright notice may be reproduced or utilized in any form or by any means, electronic or mechanical, including photocopying, recording or by any information storage and retrievable system, without written permission from the copyright holder.

To obtain permission(s) to use the material from this work for any purpose including workshops or seminars, please submit a written request to:

XAMonline, Inc.
21 Orient Avenue
Melrose, MA 02176
Toll Free 1-800-301-4647
Email: info@xamonline.com
Web: www.xamonline.com
Fax: 1-617-583-5552

Library of Congress Cataloging-in-Publication Data

Wynne, Sharon A.
    TExES Mathematics 7–12 235 Practice Test Kit: Teacher Certification /
    Sharon A. Wynne   ISBN 978-1-60787-390-7
    1. TExES Mathematics 7-12 235
    2. Study Guides
    3. TExES
    4. Teachers' Certification & Licensure
    5. Careers

Disclaimer:

The opinions expressed in this publication are the sole works of XAMonline and were created independently from the State Department of Education or other testing affiliates.

Sample test questions are developed by XAMonline and are not former tests. XAMonline makes no claims nor guarantees teacher candidates a passing score.

Printed in the United States of America

TExES Mathematics 7–12 235 Practice Test Kit
ISBN: 978-1-60787-390-7

About This Practice Test Kit

The TExES Mathematics 7–12 (235) exam is designed to ensure that certified teachers possess the necessary skills and knowledge to teach the state-approved high school mathematics curriculum in Texas public schools (the Texas Essential Knowledge and Skills [TEKS] curriculum).

As an excerpt of the TExES Mathematics 7–12 (235) study guide, this practice test kit includes two full-length practice tests that allow you to assess your skills and gauge your test readiness. Just like the actual exam, each practice test includes a total of 100 items.

Each multiple-choice question will contain from two to four response options, and you will indicate your answer by selecting A, B, C, or D.

Each question in this practice test kit includes a rigor level (Easy, Average, Rigorous) and the TExES Mathematics competency and skill (e.g., Skill 1.2) in parentheses right after each question.

Detailed answer explanations, or rationales, reference related skills in the TExES Mathematics 7–12 (235) study guide, allowing you to identify your strengths and weaknesses and master the content. Maximize your study by prioritizing the competencies and skills most in need of your focus to help you pass the exam.

Note: Some test questions for Mathematics 7–12 are designed to be solved with a graphing calculator. When you take the actual exam, an online calculator is available as part of the testing software for tests that require the use of a calculator.

Table of Contents

PRETEST 1

Answer Key and Rigor Table 18
Answers with Rationales 18

POSTTEST 53

Answer Key and Rigor Table 71
Answers with Rationales 71

PRETEST

(Average) (Skill 1.2)

1. On which of the following sets is multiplication *not* symmetric?

   A. Real numbers
   B. Complex numbers
   C. Polynomials
   D. Matrices

(Average) (Skill 1.4)

2. 6! is equal to:

   A. 6
   B. 61
   C. 120
   D. 720

(Average) (Skill 1.4)

3. $\dfrac{2^7 \times 2^8}{2^3} =$

   A. 2^4
   B. 2^6
   C. 2^{12}
   D. 2^{18}

(Easy) (Skill 1.5)

4. $2(5 + 3 \times \sqrt{25}) \div (14 - 9) \times 4 = ?$

   A. 32
   B. 20
   C. 25
   D. 40

(Average) (Skill 1.6)

5. In 10 seconds, Sharon can run 71 yards, Mary can run 83 yards, and Nancy can run 18 yards more than Sharon. How many more yards can Nancy run than Mary in 10 seconds?

   A. 6
   B. 9
   C. 12
   D. 18

(Average) (Skill 1.6)

6. Jose's class library has 220 nonfiction books and 363 fiction books. What is the ratio of nonfiction books to fiction books?

   A. 22:36
   B. 20:33
   C. 22:58
   D. 36:58

(Average) (Skill 2.1)

7. Which of the following equations have no real solutions, only complex ones?

   I. $x + 1 = 0$
   II. $x^2 + 1 = 0$
   III. $x^3 + 1 = 0$

   A. I only
   B. II only
   C. III only
   D. II and III

(Easy) (Skill 2.2)

8. A complex number that is the conjugate of itself must have:

   A. Real and imaginary parts that are equal
   B. A real part equal to zero
   C. An imaginary part equal to zero
   D. A real part that is larger than the imaginary part

(Average) (Skill 2.5)

9. Which of the following is an equivalent representation of $\frac{3-4i}{1+2i}$?

   A. 3
   B. $2 - 6i$
   C. $3 - 2i$
   D. $-1 - 2i$

(Average) (Skill 3.1)

10. What is the GCF of 143 and 156?

    A. 2
    B. 3
    C. 13
    D. No common factors

(Easy) (Skill 3.3)

11. The scalar multiplication of the number 3 with the matrix $\begin{pmatrix} 2 & 1 \\ 3 & 5 \end{pmatrix}$ yields:

    A. 33
    B. $\begin{pmatrix} 6 & 1 \\ 9 & 5 \end{pmatrix}$
    C. $\begin{pmatrix} 2 & 3 \\ 3 & 15 \end{pmatrix}$
    D. $\begin{pmatrix} 6 & 3 \\ 9 & 15 \end{pmatrix}$

(Rigorous) (Skill 3.3)

12. Evaluate the following matrix product:
    $\begin{pmatrix} 2 & 1 & 3 \\ 2 & 2 & 4 \end{pmatrix} \cdot \begin{pmatrix} 6 & 5 \\ 2 & 1 \\ 2 & 7 \end{pmatrix}$

    A. $\begin{pmatrix} 20 & 32 & 24 \\ 24 & 40 & 48 \end{pmatrix}$
    B. $\begin{pmatrix} 20 & 32 \\ 40 & 24 \\ 24 & 48 \end{pmatrix}$
    C. 116
    D. $\begin{pmatrix} 20 & 32 \\ 24 & 40 \end{pmatrix}$

(Average) (Skill 3.3)

13. Solve the following matrix equation:
    $3x + \begin{pmatrix} 1 & 5 & 2 \\ 0 & 6 & 9 \end{pmatrix} = \begin{pmatrix} 7 & 17 & 5 \\ 3 & 9 & 9 \end{pmatrix}$

    A. $\begin{pmatrix} 2 & 4 & 1 \\ 1 & 1 & 0 \end{pmatrix}$
    B. 2
    C. $\begin{pmatrix} 8 & 23 & 7 \\ 3 & 15 & 18 \end{pmatrix}$
    D. $\begin{pmatrix} 9 \\ 2 \end{pmatrix}$

(Rigorous) (Skill 3.3)

14. Find the value of the determinant of the following matrix:
    $\begin{vmatrix} 2 & 1 & -1 \\ 4 & -1 & 4 \\ 0 & -3 & 2 \end{vmatrix}$

    A. 0
    B. 23
    C. 24
    D. 40

(Average) (Skill 3.4)

15. Mercedes deposits $550.00 into a savings account that earns an annual interest rate of 3.5%. What is the balance after one year?

    A. $19.25
    B. $553.50
    C. $569.25
    D. $585.00

(Average) (Skill 3.4)

16. Dana and Megan have to fill 500 envelopes for a charity. At the end of the morning Dana has filled $\frac{3}{20}$ of the envelopes and Megan has filled $\frac{1}{4}$ of them. How many envelopes have they filled together?

    A. 75
    B. 125
    C. 200
    D. 50

(Rigorous) (Skill 3.4)

17. A scientist is measuring a physical constant that has an accepted value of 5.729 units. If the scientist's measurement is 5.693, what is his percentage error?

    A. 0.0063%
    B. 0.63%
    C. 1.79%
    D. 10%

(Average) (Skill 3.5)

18. Determine the number of subsets of set K:

    $K = \{4, 5, 6, 7\}$

    A. 15
    B. 16
    C. 17
    D. 18

(Easy) (Skill 4.1)

19. What is the shortest path between points A and B?

    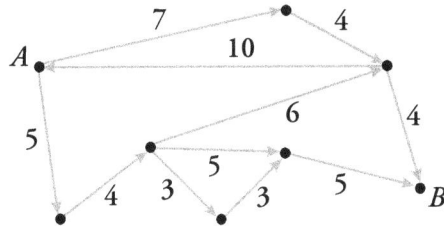

    A. 11
    B. 14
    C. 15
    D. 19

(Average) (Skill 4.2)

20. Which of the following is a recursive definition of the sequence {1, 2, 2, 4, 8, 32, ...}?

    A. $N_i = 2N_{i-1}$
    B. $N_i = 2N_{i-2}$
    C. $N_i = N_{i-1}^2$
    D. $N_i = N_{i-1}N_{i-2}$

(Easy) (Skill 4.2)

21. The Fibonacci numbers are defined recursively using the expression $F_{i+1} = F_i + F_{i-1}$. If $F_1 = 0$ and $F_2 = 1$, what is F_8?

   A. 0
   B. 1
   C. 13
   D. 21

(Rigorous) (Skill 4.4)

22. Which of the following can be used to prove that $0.\bar{9} = 1$?

   A. Arithmetic series
   B. Geometric series
   C. Fibonacci sequence
   D. Irrational numbers

(Average) (Skill 4.5)

23. If an initial deposit of $1,000 is made to a savings account with a continuously compounded annual interest rate of 5%, how much money is in the account after 4.5 years?

   A. $1,200.00
   B. $1,225.00
   C. $1,245.52
   D. $1,252.32

(Average) (Skill 5.2)

24. What is the domain of the function $g(x) = \tan x$?

   A. $\{x \in \mathbb{R}\}$
   B. $\{x \in \mathbb{R}: x \neq \pm n\pi\}$ (n odd)
   C. $\{x \in \mathbb{R}: x \neq \pm \frac{n\pi}{2}\}$ (n odd)
   D. $\{\varnothing\}$

(Average) (Skill 5.4)

25. $x^2 + 4x + 9$ is an example of:

   A. A one-to-one function
   B. An even function
   C. An odd function
   D. None of the above

(Rigorous) (Skill 5.6)

26. Find the inverse of the function $f(x) = 2x^2 - 3$.

   A. $f^{-1}(x) = \sqrt{\frac{x+3}{2}}$
   B. $f^{-1}(x) = 2x^2 + 3$
   C. $f^{-1}(x) = \sqrt{2x^2 + 3}$
   D. The function does not have an inverse

(Rigorous) (Skill 5.6)

27. Which of the following represents $f \circ g$, where $f(x) = 3x^2 + 1$ and $g(x) = 2 \sin x - 1$?

   A. $2 \sin(3x^2 + 1) - 1$
   B. $6 \sin x - 2$
   C. $3 \sin x + 1$
   D. $12 \sin^2 x - 12 \sin x + 4$

(Average) (Skill 5.6)

28. Which of the following functions does *not* have an inverse?

   A. x^3
   B. $\ln \frac{x}{2}$
   C. e^{x^2}
   D. $\frac{1}{x}$

(Easy) (Skill 6.2)

29. What is the equation of the graph shown below?

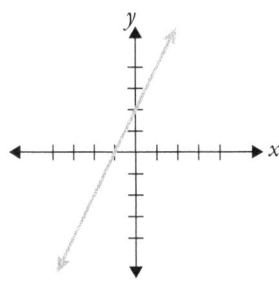

A. $2x + y = 2$
B. $2x - y = -2$
C. $2x - y = 2$
D. $2x + y = -2$

(Average) (Skill 6.6)

30. Which graph represents the solution set for $x^2 - 5x > -6$?

A.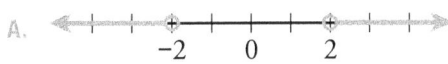

B.

C. (number line with solid segment from -2 to 2 with open circles)

D. (number line with segment between 2 and 3)

(Rigorous) (Skill 6.7)

31. Which graph shows the solution to the system of inequalities below?

$3x - 2y \leq 5$
$-x + 5y > 1$

A.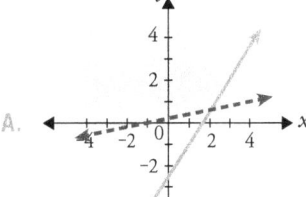

B.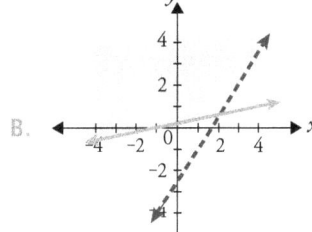

C.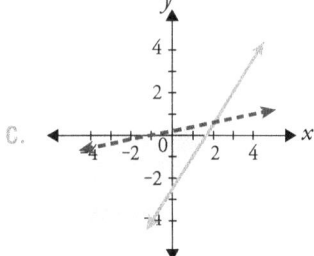

D.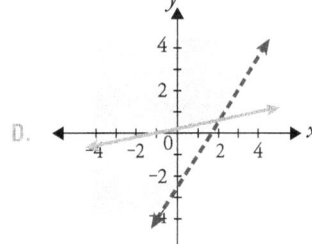

(Easy) (Skill 6.7)

32. Solve for x: $7 - 5x = 7x - 11 - 3x$.

    A. -2
    B. 2
    C. $-1\frac{1}{2}$
    D. $3\frac{1}{4}$

(Easy) (Skill 7.1)

33. Which of the following is equivalent to $\sqrt[b]{x^a}$?

    A. $x^{\frac{a}{b}}$
    B. $x^{\frac{b}{a}}$
    C. $a^{\frac{x}{b}}$
    D. $b^{\frac{x}{a}}$

(Average) (Skill 7.4)

34. The function shown in the graph below is:

    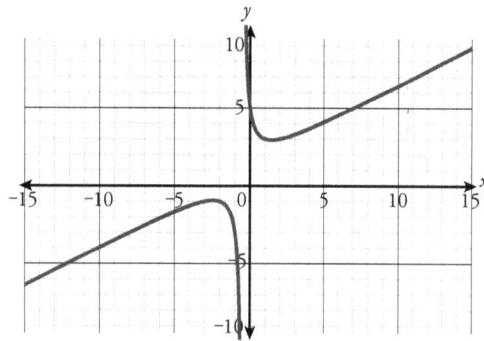

    A. $\frac{x^2 + 3x + 5}{2x^3 + 1}$
    B. $\frac{3x + 5}{2x + 1}$
    C. $\frac{x^2 + 3x + 5}{2x - 1}$
    D. $\frac{x^2 + 3x + 5}{2x + 1}$

(Rigorous) (Skill 7.6)

35. Which of the following is a factor of $6 + 48m^3$?

    A. $(1 + 2m)$
    B. $(1 - 8m)$
    C. $(1 + m - 2m)$
    D. $(1 - m + 2m)$

(Rigorous) (Skill 7.6)

36. Which expression is equal to $x^4 + 2x^3 - 16x^2 - 2x + 15$ divided by $x + 5$?

    A. $4x^3 + 6x^2 - 32x - 2$
    B. $x^3 - 15x^2 - 5x + 15$
    C. $x^3 - 3x^2 - x + 3$
    D. $5x^3 + 10x^2 - 80x + 75$

(Rigorous) (Skill 8.1)

37. Which of the following is the algebraic equivalent of the function given below in tabular form?

x	y
-2	$\frac{1}{8}$
-1	$\frac{1}{2}$
0	2
1	8
2	32

    A. $y = \frac{3}{8}x + 2$
    B. $y = 2(4^x)$
    C. $y = x^2 - \frac{31}{8}$
    D. $y = 4^x$

(Rigorous) (Skill 8.3)

38. Solve $\ln x + \ln x^2 + \ln x^3 = 3$.

    A. $e^{0.5}$

    B. $3^{\frac{1}{6}}$

    C. e^2

    D. 3^6

(Rigorous) (Skill 8.5)

39. A population P of bacteria doubles in number every hour. Which of the following functions of t in hours best represents the number of bacteria in the population?

    A. P^t

    B. $P(2^t)$

    C. Pt^2

    D. Pe^t

(Rigorous) (Skill 8.6)

40. The acidity or alkalinity of a substance is measured using the logarithmic pH scale, where the pH of a substance is given by the equation $pH = -\log_{10}[H^+]$, where $[H^+]$ is the hydrogen ion concentration in moles per liter. If the pH of a substance is 5.5, what is its hydrogen ion concentration in moles per liter?

    A. 3.16×10^{-6}

    B. 4.08×10^{-3}

    C. 3.16×10^6

    D. 4.08×10^3

(Easy) (Skill 9.5)

41. Which of the following is a Pythagorean identity?

    A. $\sin^2 \theta - \cos^2 \theta = 1$

    B. $\sin^2 \theta + \cos^2 \theta = 1$

    C. $\cos^2 \theta - \sin^2 \theta = 1$

    D. $\cos^2 \theta + \tan^2 \theta = 1$

(Easy) (Skill 9.5)

42. The cosine function is equivalent to:

    A. $\frac{1}{\text{sine}}$

    B. $\frac{1}{\text{tangent}}$

    C. $\frac{\text{sine}}{\text{tangent}}$

    D. $\frac{\text{cotangent}}{\text{sine}}$

(Rigorous) (Skill 9.6)

43. Determine the measure of the angle α in the triangle below.

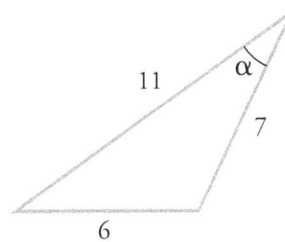

    A. 15.3°

    B. 18°

    C. 29.5°

    D. 45°

(Easy) (Skill 10.1)

44. L'Hopital's rule provides a method to evaluate which of the following?

    A. Limit of a function
    B. Derivative of a function
    C. Sum of an arithmetic series
    D. Sum of a geometric series

(Rigorous) (Skill 10.1)

45. Find the following limit: $\lim_{x \to 2} \frac{x^2 - 4}{x - 2}$.

    A. 0
    B. Infinity
    C. 2
    D. 4

(Rigorous) (Skill 10.3)

46. What is the maximum value of the function $f(x) = -3x^2 - 5$?

    A. −5
    B. −3
    C. 1
    D. 5

(Rigorous) (Skill 10.3)

47. Find the absolute maximum obtained by the function $y = 2x^2 + 3x$ on the interval $x = 0$ to $x = 3$.

    A. $-\frac{3}{4}$
    B. $-\frac{4}{3}$
    C. 0
    D. 27

(Rigorous) (Skill 10.4)

48. Find the antiderivative for $4x^3 - 2x + 6 = y$.

    A. $x^4 - x^2 + 6x + C$
    B. $x^4 - \frac{2}{3}x^3 + 6x + C$
    C. $12x^2 - 2 + C$
    D. $\frac{4}{3}x^4 - x^2 + 6x + C$

(Rigorous) (Skill 10.5)

49. The radius of a spherical balloon is increasing at a rate of 2 feet per minute. What is the rate of increase of the volume when the radius is 4 feet?

    A. 4 feet³/minute
    B. 32π feet³/minute
    C. 85.3π feet³/minute
    D. 128π feet³/minute

(Rigorous) (Skill 11.1)

50. Given that M is a mass, V is a velocity, A is an acceleration, and T is a time, what type of unit corresponds to the overall expression $\frac{AMT}{V}$?

    A. Mass
    B. Time
    C. Velocity
    D. Acceleration

(Average) (Skill 11.1)

51. The term "cubic feet" indicates which kind of measurement?

    A. Volume
    B. Mass
    C. Length
    D. Distance

(Easy) (Skill 11.1)

52. Which unit of measurement would be the most appropriate for characterizing the weight of a dime?

   A. Gram
   B. Kilogram
   C. Pound
   D. Ton

(Rigorous) (Skill 11.3)

53. When the side of a regular hexagon is doubled, its area increases by a factor of:

   A. 2
   B. 4
   C. $\frac{3}{4}$
   D. $3\sqrt{3}$

(Average) (Skill 11.4)

54. An employee of a security firm is standing on a 10-foot ladder and placing spikes on top of a fence. If the top of the ladder touches the top of the fence and the bottom of the ladder is 4 feet away from the bottom of the fence, how high is the fence?

   A. 6 ft.
   B. 14 ft.
   C. $2\sqrt{21}$ ft.
   D. $2\sqrt{29}$ ft.

(Rigorous) (Skill 12.1)

55. Which of the following is *not* true of an axiomatic system?

   A. The theorems are deduced from axioms
   B. It contains both defined and undefined terms
   C. Some axiomatic systems do not contain undefined terms
   D. All parts of an axiomatic system are consistent with each other

(Rigorous) (Skill 12.2)

56. In the figure shown below, angle $AOB = 30°$, angle $FOE = (3x - 10)°$, and angle $DOC = x°$. What is the value of x?

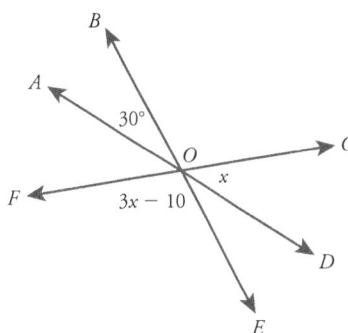

   A. 30°
   B. 40°
   C. 60°
   D. 110°

(Average) (Skill 12.3)

57. In the figure below, angles x and y are equal. From this we can conclude that:

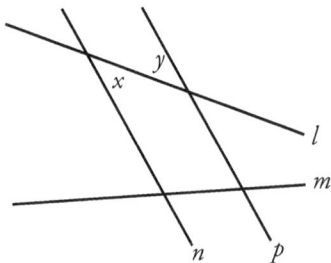

A. Lines l and m are parallel

B. Lines n and p are parallel

C. Lines m and p are perpendicular

D. Lines n and l are perpendicular

(Average) (Skill 12.4)

58. ABC and DEF are similar triangles where $\angle A = \angle D$, $\angle B = \angle E$, $\angle C = \angle F$, $AB = 5$ cm, $DE = 7.5$ cm, and $BC = 6$ cm. What is the length of EF?

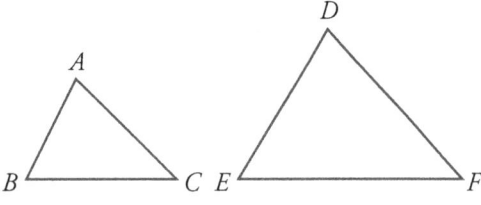

A. 9 cm

B. 4 cm

C. 6.25 cm

D. 8.5 cm

(Rigorous) (Skill 13.1)

59. Choose the correct statement concerning the median and altitude in a triangle.

A. The median and altitude of a triangle may be the same segment

B. The median and altitude of a triangle are always different segments

C. The median and altitude of a right triangle are always the same segment

D. The median and altitude of an isosceles triangle are always the same segment

(Average) (Skill 13.1)

60. Which of the following is *not* true? An equilateral triangle:

A. Has three equal sides

B. Has three equal angles

C. Has three acute angles

D. Has three obtuse angles

(Rigorous) (Skill 13.4)

61. Given a 30-by-60-meter garden with a circular fountain with a 5-meter radius, calculate the area of the portion of the garden *not* occupied by the fountain.

A. 1,721 m²

B. 1,879 m²

C. 2,585 m²

D. 1,015 m²

(Easy) (Skill 13.5)

62. The cross-section of a three-dimensional figure is circular in shape. The figure could be a:

    I. Sphere
    II. Cylinder
    III. Cone
    IV. Rectangular prism

    A. I only
    B. I and II
    C. I, II, and III
    D. I, II, III, and IV

(Rigorous) (Skill 14.4)

63. A figure placed in quadrant II of the *x-y* coordinate plane is rotated 90° counterclockwise about the origin in the *x-y* plane and then reflected in the *x*-axis. The final position of the figure is in:

    A. Quadrant I
    B. Quadrant II
    C. Quadrant III
    D. Quadrant IV

(Rigorous) (Skill 14.5)

64. Two points have coordinates (3, -4, 1) and (6, 2, -7). What is the distance between these points?

    A. 7 units
    B. 10.4 units
    C. 13.5 units
    D. 15 units

(Rigorous) (Skill 14.6)

65. What are the foci of the ellipse $16(y-3)^2 = 16 - (x-2)^2$?

    A. $(2 \pm 4, 3)$
    B. $(-2 \pm \sqrt{15}, -3)$
    C. $(2 \pm \sqrt{15}, 3)$
    D. $(2, 3 \pm \sqrt{15})$

(Rigorous) (Skill 14.7)

66. Which of the following best describes the translation matrix below for arbitrary points (x_1, y_1)?

    $$\begin{pmatrix} 1 & 0 \\ 0 & -1 \end{pmatrix} \begin{pmatrix} x_1 \\ y_1 \end{pmatrix} = \begin{pmatrix} x_2 \\ y_2 \end{pmatrix}$$

    A. Rotation
    B. Translation
    C. Reflection
    D. Dilation

(Rigorous) (Skill 14.8)

67. Determine the rectangular coordinates of the point with polar coordinates (5, 60°).

    A. (0.5, 0.87)
    B. (-0.5, 0.87)
    C. (2.5, 4.33)
    D. (25, 150°)

(Average) (Skill 15.2)

68. Which of the following types of graphs would *not* be used to record the eye color of the students in the class?

    A. Bar graph
    B. Line graph
    C. Pictograph
    D. Circle graph

(Easy) (Skill 15.2)

69. What conclusion can be drawn from the graph below?

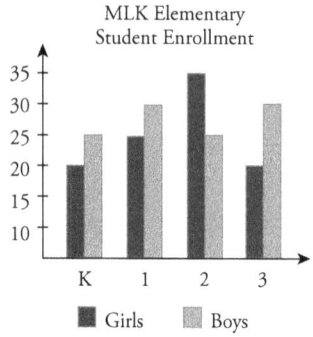

A. The number of students in first grade exceeds the number in second grade

B. There are more boys than girls in the entire school

C. There are more girls than boys in the first grade

D. Third grade has the largest number of students

(Easy) (Skill 15.2)

70. The pie chart below shows sales at an automobile dealership for the first four months of a year. What percentage of the vehicles were sold in April?

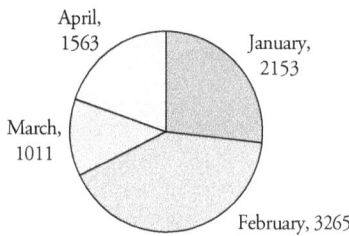

A. More than 50%

B. Less than 25%

C. Between 25% and 50%

D. None

Easy) (Skill 15.3)

71. Which word best describes a set of measured values that are all very similar but deviate significantly from the expected result?

A. Perfect

B. Precise

C. Accurate

D. Appropriate

(Average) (Skill 15.3)

72. An archer's paper target shows the hits illustrated below. Which term best describes the archer's shooting in this case?

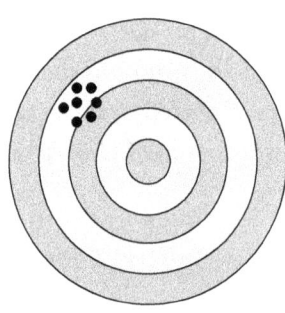

A. Accurate

B. Precise

C. Exact

D. On target

(Easy) (Skill 15.4)

73. Compute the median for the following data set:

{12, 19, 13, 16, 17, 14}

A. 14.5

B. 15.17

C. 15

D. 16

(Rigorous) (Skill 15.4)

74. What is the standard deviation of the following sample?

    {1.46, 1.55, 1.55, 1.57, 1.89, 2.01, 2.09}

    A. 0.010
    B. 0.066
    C. 0.26
    D. 1.73

(Rigorous) (Skill 15.4)

75. Which measure of central tendency best characterizes the data set below?

Value	Frequency
1	2
2	5
3	7
4	3
5	2
6	1
7	1

    A. Mean
    B. Median
    C. Both the mean and median are the same
    D. None of the above

(Rigorous) (Skill 16.2)

76. How many different five-card hands containing three aces and two kings can be drawn from a standard 52-card deck?

    A. 6
    B. 16
    C. 24
    D. 2,598,960

(Average) (Skill 16.3)

77. What is the probability that a roll of a six-sided die yields an outcome that is even or greater than three?

    A. $\frac{3}{6}$
    B. $\frac{4}{6}$
    C. $\frac{5}{6}$
    D. 1

(Easy) (Skill 16.3)

78. On the throw of a six-sided die, what is the probability that you will roll a number less than three?

    A. $\frac{1}{2}$
    B. $\frac{1}{6}$
    C. $\frac{1}{3}$
    D. $\frac{2}{3}$

(Rigorous) (Skill 16.4)

79. Three identical green chairs and four identical red chairs are randomly arranged in a single row. What is the probability that no chair will be placed next to one of the same color?

    A. $\frac{1}{7}$
    B. $\frac{1}{35}$
    C. $\frac{3}{7}$
    D. $\frac{3}{35}$

(Rigorous) (Skill 16.6)

80. A baseball team has a 60% chance of winning any particular game in a 7-game series. What is the probability that it will win the series by winning games 6 and 7?

   A. 8.3%

   B. 36%

   C. 50%

   D. 60%

(Easy) (Skill 17.1)

81. In a statistical experiment, a sample is:

   A. The total set of possible observations

   B. A single observation

   C. A set of observations selected from the population

   D. None of the above

(Average) (Skill 17.4)

82. The height of people in a certain city is a normally distributed random variable. If a person is chosen from the city at random, what is the probability that he or she has a height greater than the mean of the distribution?

   A. 0.25

   B. 0.5

   C. 0.75

   D. Not enough information

(Average) (Skill 17.5)

83. Which of the following is the best kind of function for a regression fit of the data shown in the plot below?

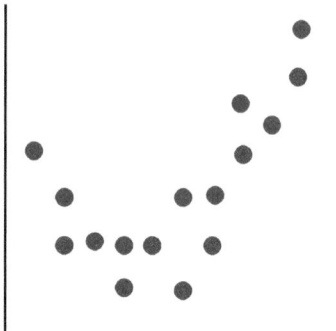

   A. Linear

   B. Quadratic

   C. Exponential

   D. Logarithmic

(Average) (Skill 17.7)

84. According to the central limit theorem:

   A. The larger the sample size, the closer the sample mean is to the population mean

   B. The larger the sample size, the closer the correlation coefficient is to 1

   C. As the number of samples increases, the correlation coefficient is closer to 1

   D. As the number of samples increases, the distribution of sample means approaches a normal distribution

(Average) (Skill 17.8)

85. Of 75 students surveyed in a school, 50 had perfect attendance for the year. Estimate the fraction of students in the entire school that had perfect attendance using a point estimator from the given sample.

    A. $\frac{2}{3}$

    B. 66%

    C. $\frac{5}{7}$

    D. $\frac{1}{3}$

(Average) (Skill 18.1)

86. Which of the following are valid methods of mathematical proof?

    I. Show that the conclusion follows necessarily from the premises by going through logical steps, each of which follows from the previous step.

    II. Disprove a statement by providing a single counterexample.

    III. Prove a statement by showing that assuming it to be false leads to a contradiction.

    A. I and II

    B. I and III

    C. II and III

    D. I, II, and III

(Average) (Skill 18.2)

87. Let x, y, and z represent mathematical statements. Which of the following is a valid conclusion based on the premises given below?

    I. If x, then y
    II. If y, then z

    A. If x, then z

    B. If z, then x

    C. If y, then x

    D. If z, then y

(Average) (Skill 19.1)

88. A student is given the angle measures of two similar triangles ABC and DEF and the lengths of some of the sides. He is asked to find the lengths of the other sides. What would be a good first step in approaching this problem?

    A. Make a list of the steps to be used to solve the problem

    B. Guess the lengths and check if the proportions are correct

    C. Draw a diagram showing the two labeled triangles and side lengths

    D. Try to first find the solution to a simpler problem

(Rigorous) (Skill 18.6)

89. A student makes temperature measurements outdoors starting at 10 a.m. and ending at 2 p.m. The temperature is 50°F at 10 a.m. and increases by about 1°F every half hour. She sets up a mathematical model to represent her observations. Which of the following is an incorrect use of the model?

    A. The equation $T = 50 + 2h$ is written to represent the temperature between 10 a.m. and 2 p.m.
    B. Using the model, the temperature is estimated to be 52.5°F at 11:15 a.m.
    C. Using the model, the temperature is estimated to be 66°F at 6 p.m.
    D. None of the above

(Average) (Skill 19.1)

90. Students in a classroom are led through an activity in which they fold a sheet of paper in half, fold it again to halve the area, and keep folding it in successive halves as many times as they can. They are usually surprised to discover that the piece of paper gets really small after just a few folds. This exercise is used to represent the mathematical concept of:

    A. Proportional reasoning
    B. Percentage
    C. The area of a rectangle
    D. The exponential function

(Average) (Skill 19.3)

91. Which words in a test problem would indicate that an addition operation is needed?

    A. Each
    B. How many
    C. In each group
    D. How many more than

(Rigorous) (Skill 19.4)

92. What is the main purpose of having kindergarten students count by twos?

    A. To hear a rhythm
    B. To recognize patterns in numbers
    C. To practice addition
    D. To become familiar with equations

(Average) (Skill 19.6)

93. What is the correct mathematical term for the distance from the origin to a point on a graph where a straight line crosses the x-axis or y-axis?

    A. Cutoff point
    B. Intercept
    C. Slope
    D. Asymptote

(Easy) (Skill 20.2)

94. The best way to help a visual learner understand a mathematical problem is to:

    A. Draw a diagram to represent the problem
    B. Explain the problem in simple words
    C. Provide manipulatives to model the problem
    D. Allow the student to move around while working on the problem

(Rigorous) (Skill 20.6)

95. When a student completes the following number sentence, which mathematical concept is being learned?

    $15 - x = 6$

    A. Addition/subtraction and basic algebraic concepts

    B. Counting and addition/subtraction

    C. Counting and basic algebraic concepts

    D. Counting and pattern recognition

(Rigorous) (Skill 20.6)

96. Students completing an activity with tangrams are learning which mathematical principle?

    A. Basic geometric concepts

    B. Repeating patterns

    C. Counting

    D. Identity property

(Rigorous) (Skill 20.6)

97. Kindergarten students are participating in a calendar time activity. One student adds a straw to the "ones can" to represent that day of school. Which mathematical principle is being reinforced?

    A. Properties of a base ten number system

    B. Sorting

    C. Counting by twos

    D. Even and odd numbers

(Average) (Skill 20.6)

98. The purpose of a formative assessment is to:

    A. Provide parents and school with an intermediate progress report

    B. Assess learning outcomes for a certain time period

    C. Provide feedback to the student and teacher to help the student improve

    D. Test the validity of the assessment method

(Average) (Skill 21.2)

99. An assessment must *not*:

    A. Be based on material taught in class

    B. Ask students to use mathematical methods familiar to them

    C. Be similar to homework problems

    D. Consist of unfamiliar material to assess how well students can think on their feet

(Rigorous) (Skill 21.3)

100. In a geometry assessment, the teacher provides a verbal description of a problem and does not include a diagram. What is the most likely reason for this omission?

    A. The teacher wishes to test the students' ability to accurately translate the verbal description to a diagram

    B. Creating a diagram would take too much effort

    C. The problem is a test of mathematical terminology

    D. The teacher wishes to raise the difficulty level of the problem

Pretest Answer Key

1. D	11. D	21. C	31. A	41. B	51. A	61. A	71. B	81. C	91. B
2. D	12. D	22. B	32. B	42. C	52. A	62. C	72. B	82. B	92. B
3. C	13. A	23. D	33. A	43. C	53. B	63. B	73. C	83. B	93. B
4. A	14. C	24. C	34. D	44. A	54. C	64. B	74. C	84. D	94. A
5. A	15. C	25. D	35. A	45. D	55. C	65. C	75. A	85. A	95. A
6. B	16. C	26. D	36. C	46. A	56. B	66. C	76. C	86. D	96. A
7. B	17. B	27. D	37. B	47. D	57. B	67. C	77. B	87. A	97. A
8. C	18. B	28. C	38. A	48. A	58. A	68. B	78. C	88. C	98. C
9. D	19. C	29. B	39. B	49. D	59. A	69. B	79. B	89. C	99. D
10. C	20. D	30. D	40. A	50. A	60. D	70. B	80. A	90. D	100. A

Pretest Rigor Table

Rigor level	Questions
Easy 20%	4, 8, 11, 19, 21, 29, 32, 33, 41, 42, 44, 52, 62, 69, 70, 71, 73, 78, 81, 94
Average 40%	1, 2, 3, 5, 6, 7, 9, 10, 13, 15, 16, 18, 20, 23, 24, 25, 28, 30, 34, 51, 54, 57, 58, 59, 60, 68, 72, 77, 82, 83, 84, 85, 86, 87, 88, 90, 91, 93, 98, 99
Rigorous 40%	12, 14, 17, 22, 26, 27, 31, 35, 36, 37, 38, 39, 40, 43, 45, 46, 47, 48, 49, 50, 53, 55, 56, 61, 63, 64, 65, 66, 67, 74, 75, 76, 79, 80, 89, 92, 95, 96, 97, 100

Pretest Answers with Rationales

(Average) (Skill 1.2)

1. On which of the following sets is multiplication *not* symmetric?

    A. Real numbers

    B. Complex numbers

    C. Polynomials

    D. Matrices

Answer: D. Matrices

A binary relation R is symmetric on a set if, for all a and b in a set, both aRb and bRa have the same truth value. For real numbers, complex numbers and polynomials with members a and b in each case, ab is always equal to ba. For matrices, however, ab is not always equal to ba for given matrices a and b. Thus, the correct answer is D.

(Average) (Skill 1.4)

2. 6! is equal to:

    A. 6

    B. 61

    C. 120

    D. 720

Answer: D. 720

6! is 6 factorial, which is defined as $6! = 6 \times 5 \times 4 \times 3 \times 2 \times 1 = 720$.

(Average) (Skill 1.4)

3. $\frac{2^7 \times 2^8}{2^3} =$

    A. 2^4

    B. 2^6

    C. 2^{12}

    D. 2^{18}

Answer: C. 2^{12}

The rules for multiplying and dividing terms with exponents are:

$a^m \times a^n = a^{m+n}$; $\frac{a^m}{a^n} = a^{m-n}$

So, $\frac{2^7 \times 2^8}{2^3} = \frac{2^{7+8}}{2^3} = \frac{2^{15}}{2^3} = 2^{15-3} = 2^{12}$.

(Easy) (Skill 1.5)

4. $2(5 + 3 \times \sqrt{25}) \div (14 - 9) \times 4 = ?$

    A. 32

    B. 20

    C. 25

    D. 40

Answer: A. 32

First perform the operations inside parentheses, doing multiplication before addition: $5 + 3 \times \sqrt{25} = 5 + 3 \times 5 = 5 + 15 = 20$ and $14 - 9 = 5$. This gives $2(5 + 3 \times \sqrt{25}) \div (14 - 9) \times 4 = 2(20) \div 5 \times 4$.

Now do the multiplications and divisions from left to right: $2(20) \div 5 \times 4 = 40 \div 5 \times 4 = 8 \times 4 = 32$.

(Average) (Skill 1.6)

5. In 10 seconds, Sharon can run 71 yards, Mary can run 83 yards, and Nancy can run 18 yards more than Sharon. How many more yards can Nancy run than Mary in 10 seconds?

   A. 6
   B. 9
   C. 12
   D. 18

Answer: A. 6

This is a two-step problem. First find out how many yards Nancy runs. Then how many more yards she runs than Mary. Since Nancy runs 18 more yards than Sharon and Sharon runs 71 yards in 10 seconds, Nancy runs 71 + 18 = 89 yards in 10 seconds. Mary runs 83 yards and Nancy runs 89 yards in 10 seconds. So Nancy runs 89 − 83 = 6 yards more than Mary in 10 seconds.

(Average) (Skill 1.6)

6. Jose's class library has 220 nonfiction books and 363 fiction books. What is the ratio of nonfiction books to fiction books?

   A. 22:36
   B. 20:33
   C. 22:58
   D. 36:58

Answer: B. 20:33

The ratio of nonfiction books to fiction books is 220:363. A common factor of both numbers is 11. Divide each number by 11, and the reduced ratio is 20:33.

(Average) (Skill 2.1)

7. Which of the following equations have no real solutions, only complex ones?

   I. $x + 1 = 0$
   II. $x^2 + 1 = 0$
   III. $x^3 + 1 = 0$

   A. I only
   B. II only
   C. III only
   D. II and III

Answer: B. II only

The solution to $x + 1 = 0$ is simply $x = -1$, a real number. $x^3 + 1$ can be factored as follows: $x^3 + 1 = (x + 1)(x^2 - x + 1)$. So $x^3 + 1 = 0$ has at least one real solution, $x = -1$. In Option B we have $x^2 + 1 = 0 \Rightarrow x^2 = -1 \Rightarrow x = \pm i$, both complex solutions.

(Easy) (Skill 2.2)

8. A complex number that is the conjugate of itself must have:

   A. Real and imaginary parts that are equal
   B. A real part equal to zero
   C. An imaginary part equal to zero
   D. A real part that is larger than the imaginary part

Answer: C. An imaginary part equal to zero

The complex conjugate of $a + ib$ is $a - ib$. The only condition under which these can be equal is when the imaginary part $b = 0$.

(Average) (Skill 2.5)

9. Which of the following is an equivalent representation of $\frac{3-4i}{1+2i}$?

   A. 3

   B. $2 - 6i$

   C. $3 - 2i$

   D. $-1 - 2i$

Answer: D. $-1 - 2i$

Multiply both the numerator and denominator by the complex conjugate of the denominator $(1 + 2i)$ to simplify this complex division.

$\frac{3-4i}{1+2i} \cdot \frac{1-2i}{1-2i} = \frac{3 - 6i - 4i + 8i^2}{1 - 2i + 2i - 4i^2} = \frac{-5 - 10i}{1 + 4}$
$= \frac{-5 - 10i}{5} = -1 - 2i.$

(Average) (Skill 3.1)

10. What is the GCF of 143 and 156?

    A. 2

    B. 3

    C. 13

    D. No common factors

Answer: C. 13

One way to determine the greatest common factor is to find the prime factorization (the factorization of the number in terms of prime numbers only) of each number. A strategy for prime factorization for small numbers such as those given in this question is to test each prime, starting with 2 and increasing, as a factor of the number.

$156 = 2 \times 78 = 2 \times 2 \times 39 = 2 \times 2 \times 3 \times 13$
$143 = 11 \times 13$

Note that these two numbers share only one common factor: 13. Thus, 13 is the GCF.

(Easy) (Skill 3.3)

11. The scalar multiplication of the number 3 with the matrix $\begin{pmatrix} 2 & 1 \\ 3 & 5 \end{pmatrix}$ yields:

    A. 33

    B. $\begin{pmatrix} 6 & 1 \\ 9 & 5 \end{pmatrix}$

    C. $\begin{pmatrix} 2 & 3 \\ 3 & 15 \end{pmatrix}$

    D. $\begin{pmatrix} 6 & 3 \\ 9 & 15 \end{pmatrix}$

Answer: D. $\begin{pmatrix} 6 & 3 \\ 9 & 15 \end{pmatrix}$

In scalar multiplication of a matrix by a number, each element of the matrix is multiplied by that number.

(Rigorous) (Skill 3.3)

12. Evaluate the following matrix product:
$\begin{pmatrix} 2 & 1 & 3 \\ 2 & 2 & 4 \end{pmatrix} \cdot \begin{pmatrix} 6 & 5 \\ 2 & 1 \\ 2 & 7 \end{pmatrix}$

    A. $\begin{pmatrix} 20 & 32 & 24 \\ 24 & 40 & 48 \end{pmatrix}$

    B. $\begin{pmatrix} 20 & 32 \\ 40 & 24 \\ 24 & 48 \end{pmatrix}$

    C. 116

    D. $\begin{pmatrix} 20 & 32 \\ 24 & 40 \end{pmatrix}$

Answer: D. $\begin{pmatrix} 20 & 32 \\ 24 & 40 \end{pmatrix}$

The product of a 2 × 3 matrix with a 3 × 2 matrix is a 2 × 2 matrix. This alone should be enough to identify the correct answer. Each term in the 2 × 2 matrix is calculated as follows:

Matrix 1, row 1, multiplied by matrix 2, column 1, yields entry 1, 1: 2 × 6 + 1 × 2 + 3 × 2 = 12 + 2 + 6 = 20,

Matrix 1, row 1, multiplied by matrix 2, column 2, yields entry 1, 2: 2 × 5 + 1 × 1 + 3 × 7 = 10 + 1 + 21 = 32.

Matrix 1, row 2, multiplied by matrix 2, column 1, yields entry 2, 1: 2 × 6 + 2 × 2 + 4 × 2 = 12 + 4 + 8 = 24.

Matrix 1, row 2, multiplied by matrix 2, column 2, yields entry 2, 2: 2 × 5 + 2 × 1 + 4 × 7 = 10 + 2 + 28 = 40.

(Average) (Skill 3.3)

13. **Solve the following matrix equation:**

$$3x + \begin{pmatrix} 1 & 5 & 2 \\ 0 & 6 & 9 \end{pmatrix} = \begin{pmatrix} 7 & 17 & 5 \\ 3 & 9 & 9 \end{pmatrix}$$

A. $\begin{pmatrix} 2 & 4 & 1 \\ 1 & 1 & 0 \end{pmatrix}$

B. 2

C. $\begin{pmatrix} 8 & 23 & 7 \\ 3 & 15 & 18 \end{pmatrix}$

D. $\begin{pmatrix} 9 \\ 2 \end{pmatrix}$

Answer: A. $\begin{pmatrix} 2 & 4 & 1 \\ 1 & 1 & 0 \end{pmatrix}$

Use the basic rules of algebra and matrices.

$$3x = \begin{pmatrix} 7 & 17 & 5 \\ 3 & 9 & 9 \end{pmatrix} - \begin{pmatrix} 1 & 5 & 2 \\ 0 & 6 & 9 \end{pmatrix} = \begin{pmatrix} 6 & 12 & 3 \\ 3 & 3 & 0 \end{pmatrix}$$

$$x = \frac{1}{3}\begin{pmatrix} 6 & 12 & 3 \\ 3 & 3 & 0 \end{pmatrix} = \begin{pmatrix} 2 & 4 & 1 \\ 1 & 1 & 0 \end{pmatrix}$$

(Rigorous) (Skill 3.3)

14. **Find the value of the determinant of the following matrix:**

$$\begin{vmatrix} 2 & 1 & -1 \\ 4 & -1 & 4 \\ 0 & -3 & 2 \end{vmatrix}$$

A. 0

B. 23

C. 24

D. 40

Answer: C. 24

To find the determinant of a matrix without the use of a graphing calculator, repeat the first two columns as shown:

2	1	-1	2	1
4	-1	4	4	-1
0	-3	2	0	-3

Starting with the uppermost left entry (2), multiply the three numbers in the diagonal going down to the right: 2(-1)(2) = -4. Do the same starting with 1: 1(4)(0) = 0. Repeat starting with -1: -1(4)(-3) = 12. Adding these three numbers yields 8. Repeat the same process starting with the uppermost right entry, 1. That is, multiply the three numbers in the diagonal going down to the left: 1(4)(2) = 8. Do the same starting with 2: 2(4)(-3) = -24. Repeat starting with -1: -1(-1)(0) = 0. Add these together to get -16. To find the determinant, subtract the second result from the first: 8 − (-16) = 24.

ANSWERS WITH RATIONALES

(Average) (Skill 3.4)

15. Mercedes deposits $550.00 into a savings account that earns an annual interest rate of 3.5%. What is the balance after one year?

    A. $19.25
    B. $553.50
    C. $569.25
    D. $585.00

Answer: C. $569.25

First find the interest earned, then add the interest to the amount invested. The interest is 3.5% of $550.00, or 0.035 × 550, which equals 19.25. To find the balance, add the interest, $19.25, to the amount invested, $550. The answer is $569.25.

(Average) (Skill 3.4)

16. Dana and Megan have to fill 500 envelopes for a charity. At the end of the morning Dana has filled $\frac{3}{20}$ of the envelopes and Megan has filled $\frac{1}{4}$ of them. How many envelopes have they filled together?

    A. 75
    B. 125
    C. 200
    D. 50

Answer: C. 200

The fraction of envelopes Dana and Megan have filled together = $\frac{3}{20} + \frac{1}{4}$. Expressing this sum in terms of the common denominator 20, $\frac{3}{20} + \frac{1}{4} = \frac{3}{20} + \frac{5}{20} = \frac{8}{20} = \frac{2}{5}$. $\frac{2}{5}$ of 500 = $(\frac{2}{5}) \times 500 = 200$. So Dana and Megan have filled 200 envelopes together.

(Rigorous) (Skill 3.4)

17. A scientist is measuring a physical constant that has an accepted value of 5.729 units. If the scientist's measurement is 5.693, what is his percentage error?

    A. 0.0063%
    B. 0.63%
    C. 1.79%
    D. 10%

Answer: B. 0.63%

To calculate the percentage error P, divide the absolute difference between the theoretical (accepted) value T and the experimental value E by the accepted value T, then multiply by 100%.

$$P = \frac{|E - T|}{T} \cdot 100\%$$
$$= \frac{|5.693 - 5.729|}{5.729} \cdot 100\% \approx 0.63\%$$

PRETEST

(Average) (Skill 3.5)

18. Determine the number of subsets of set K:

    $K = \{4, 5, 6, 7\}$

    A. 15
    B. 16
    C. 17
    D. 18

Answer: B. 16

A set of n objects has 2^n subsets. Therefore, here we have $2^4 = 16$ subsets. These subsets include four which each have one element only, six which each have two elements, four which each have three elements, plus the original set and the empty set.

(Easy) (Skill 4.1)

19. What is the shortest path between points A and B?

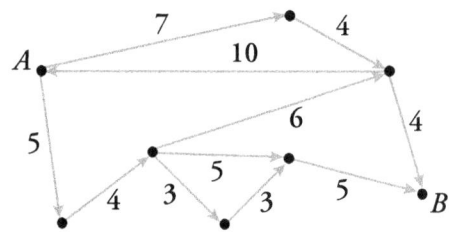

    A. 11
    B. 14
    C. 15
    D. 19

Answer: C. 15

When finding the shortest path, be sure to follow the paths in the appropriate directions. Only several direct (that is, noncircular) paths are possible; of these, the shortest path has a length of 15. This path is shown below.

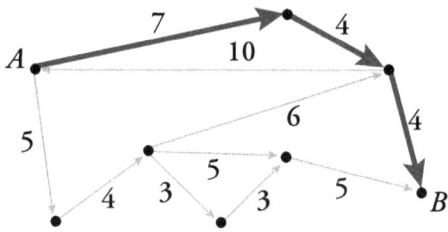

(Average) (Skill 4.2)

20. Which of the following is a recursive definition of the sequence $\{1, 2, 2, 4, 8, 32, \ldots\}$?

    A. $N_i = 2N_{i-1}$
    B. $N_i = 2N_{i-2}$
    C. $N_i = N_{i-1}^2$
    D. $N_i = N_{i-1}N_{i-2}$

Answer: D. $N_i = N_{i-1}N_{i-2}$

Test each answer or look at the pattern of the numbers in the sequence. Note that each number (with the exception of the first two) is the product of the preceding two numbers. In recursive form using index i, the expression is $N_i = N_{i-1}N_{i-2}$.

(Easy) (Skill 4.2)

21. The Fibonacci numbers are defined recursively using the expression $F_{i+1} = F_i + F_{i-1}$. If $F_1 = 0$ and $F_2 = 1$, what is F_8?

    A. 0
    B. 1
    C. 13
    D. 21

Answer: C. 13

The recursive expression simply states that each Fibonacci number is the sum of the previous two numbers. Thus, if we start with zero and one, then the Fibonacci numbers are {0, 1, 1, 2, 3, 5, 8, 13, 21,…}. On the basis of these results, F_8 is 13.

(Rigorous) (Skill 4.4)

22. Which of the following can be used to prove that $0.\overline{9} = 1$?

    A. Arithmetic series
    B. Geometric series
    C. Fibonacci sequence
    D. Irrational numbers

Answer: B. Geometric series

The number 0.9999… can be represented using a geometric series, as shown below.

$$0.\overline{9} = 9 \cdot \frac{1}{10} + 9 \cdot \frac{1}{100} + 9 \cdot \frac{1}{1,000} + \ldots$$
$$= 9\left[\left(\frac{1}{10}\right)^1 + \left(\frac{1}{10}\right)^2 + \left(\frac{1}{10}\right)^3 + \ldots\right]$$
$$0.\overline{9} = \frac{9}{10}\left[\left(\frac{1}{10}\right)^0 + \left(\frac{1}{10}\right)^1 + \left(\frac{1}{10}\right)^2 + \ldots\right]$$

But the series in brackets is simply a geometric series. We can use the following, which applies to $r < 1$, to write the series above in closed form.

$$1 + r + r^2 + r^3 + \ldots = \frac{1}{1-r}$$

Thus,

$$0.\overline{9} = \frac{9}{10}\left(\frac{1}{1-0.1}\right) = \frac{9}{10}\left(\frac{1}{0.9}\right) = \frac{9}{10}\left(\frac{10}{9}\right) = 1$$

A geometric series can therefore be used to prove that $0.\overline{9} = 1$.

(Average) (Skill 4.5)

23. If an initial deposit of $1,000 is made to a savings account with a continuously compounded annual interest rate of 5%, how much money is in the account after 4.5 years?

    A. $1,200.00
    B. $1,225.00
    C. $1,245.52
    D. $1,252.32

Answer: D. $1,252.32

Use the formula for continually compounded interest: $A = Pe^{rt}$ where A is the amount in an account with a principal of P and annual interest rate r compounded continually for t years. Then:

$$A = \$1,000 e^{0.05 \cdot 4.5} = \$1,252.32$$

(Average) (Skill 5.2)

24. What is the domain of the function $g(x) = \tan x$?

    A. $\{x \in \mathbb{R}\}$
    B. $\{x \in \mathbb{R}: x \neq \pm n\pi\}$ (n odd)
    C. $\{x \in \mathbb{R}: x \neq \pm\frac{n\pi}{2}\}$ (n odd)
    D. $\{\emptyset\}$

Answer: C. $\{x \in \mathbb{R}: x \neq \pm\frac{n\pi}{2}\}$ (n odd)

Trigonometric functions are periodic, so we know that any values not in the domain of the tangent function will occur with some periodicity. One approach to the problem is to take a look at the graph of the function to get an idea of its behavior.

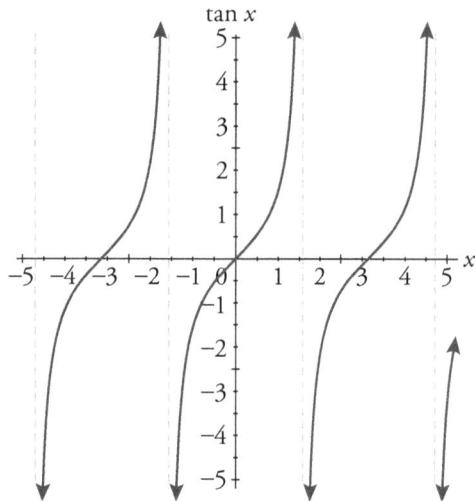

Note that the asymptotes (shown as vertical lines) show up at $-\frac{3\pi}{2}, -\frac{\pi}{2}, \frac{\pi}{2}$, and so on. Again, because the tangent function is periodic, we can say that the vertical asymptotes occur at $x = \pm\frac{n\pi}{2}$ for all odd integers n. Thus, the domain of the function is all real x where $x \neq \pm\frac{n\pi}{2}$. We can denote this as shown in Option C.

(Average) (Skill 5.4)

25. $x^2 + 4x + 9$ is an example of:

   A. A one-to-one function
   B. An even function
   C. An odd function
   D. None of the above

Answer: D. None of the above

A function is one-to-one only if it passes both the horizontal and vertical line tests, i.e., no horizontal or vertical line superimposed on the graph will cut the graph at more than one point. Since the graph of $f(x) = x^2 + 4x + 9$ is a parabolic curve, it is clearly not a one-to-one function. A function $f(x)$ is even if $f(-x) = f(x)$ and odd if $f(-x) = -f(x)$.

For $f(x) = x^2 + 4x + 9$, $f(-x) = x^2 - 4x + 9$. This does not satisfy the condition for an odd or even function.

(Rigorous) (Skill 5.6)

26. **Find the inverse of the function $f(x) = 2x^2 - 3$.**

   A. $f^{-1}(x) = \sqrt{\frac{x+3}{2}}$
   B. $f^{-1}(x) = 2x^2 + 3$
   C. $f^{-1}(x) = \sqrt{2x^2 + 3}$
   D. The function does not have an inverse

Answer: D. The function does not have an inverse

A function has an inverse if and only if it is one-to-one. A one-to-one function is a function that satisfies both the horizontal and vertical line tests (if it is a function, then by definition it already satisfies the vertical line test). Let's take a look at the graph of this function.

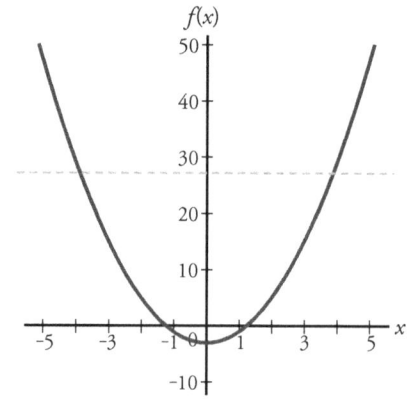

Note that the function does not satisfy the horizontal line test (two unique x values produce the same value of the function f). Thus, this function has no inverse.

(Rigorous) (Skill 5.6)

27. Which of the following represents $f \circ g$, where $f(x) = 3x^2 + 1$ and $g(x) = 2 \sin x - 1$?

   A. $2 \sin(3x^2 + 1) - 1$
   B. $6 \sin x - 2$
   C. $3 \sin x + 1$
   D. $12 \sin^2 x - 12 \sin x + 4$

Answer: D. $12 \sin^2 x - 12 \sin x + 4$

The expression $f \circ g$ represents the composition of functions $f(g(x))$. Thus, we can find $f \circ g$ by simply substituting $g(x)$ for the argument in $f(x)$.

$f \circ g = f(g(x)) = 3(2 \sin x - 1)^2 + 1 = 3(4 \sin^2 x - 4 \sin x + 1) + 1$

$f \circ g = f(g(x)) = 12 \sin^2 x - 12 \sin x + 3 + 1 = 12 \sin^2 x - 12 \sin x + 4$

Thus, the composite in this case is $12 \sin^2 x - 12 \sin x + 4$.

(Average) (Skill 5.6)

28. Which of the following functions does *not* have an inverse?

   A. x^3
   B. $\ln \frac{x}{2}$
   C. e^{x^2}
   D. $\frac{1}{x}$

Answer: C. e^{x^2}

For a function to have an inverse, it must be one-to-one. A simple way to test a function is to apply the horizontal and vertical line tests. If there exists either a horizontal or vertical line that intersects the plot of the function (or relation, more generally), then it is not one-to-one and therefore does not have an inverse. For options A, B, and D, the functions all pass the horizontal and vertical line tests. Note below, however, that the function in Option C fails the horizontal line test.

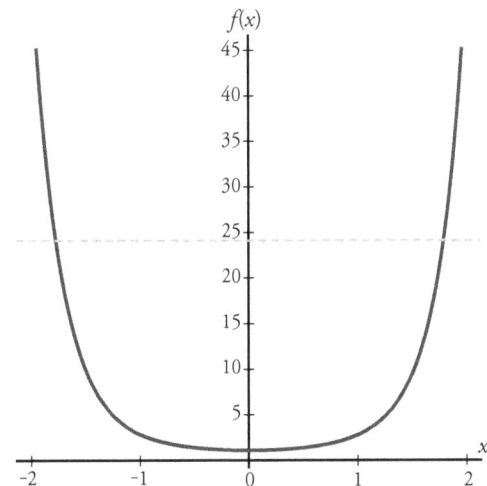

(Easy) (Skill 6.2)

29. What is the equation of the graph shown below?

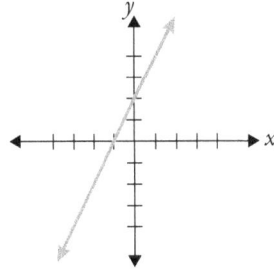

   A. $2x + y = 2$
   B. $2x - y = -2$
   C. $2x - y = 2$
   D. $2x + y = -2$

Answer: B. $2x - y = -2$

By observation, we see that the graph has a y-intercept of 2 and a slope of $\frac{2}{1} = 2$. Therefore, its equation is $y = mx + b = 2x + 2$. Rearranging the terms yields $2x - y = -2$.

(Average) (Skill 6.6)

30. Which graph represents the solution set for $x^2 - 5x > -6$?

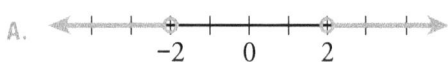

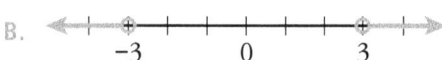

Answer: D.

Rewriting the inequality yields $x^2 - 5x + 6 > 0$. Factoring yields $(x - 2)(x - 3) > 0$.

The two cutoff points on the number line are now at $x = 2$ and $x = 3$. Choosing a random number in each of the three parts of the number line, test them to see if they produce a true statement. If $x = 0$ or $x = 4$, $(x - 2)(x - 3) > 0$ is true. If $x = 2.5$, $(x - 2)(x - 3) > 0$ is false. Therefore, the solution set is all numbers smaller than 2 or greater than 3.

(Rigorous) (Skill 6.7)

31. Which graph shows the solution to the system of inequalities below?

$3x - 2y \leq 5$
$-x + 5y > 1$

A.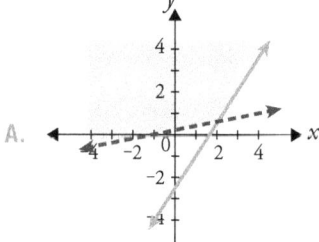

B.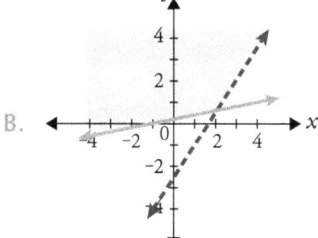

C.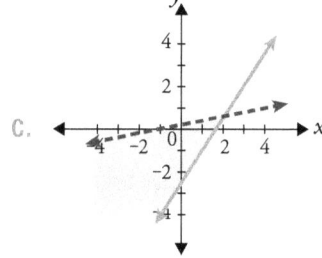

D.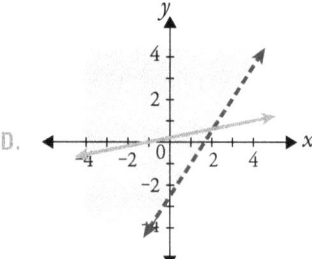

Answer: A.

First, solve each inequality for y, as shown below.

$3x - 2y \leq 5$
$2y + 5 \geq 3x$
$2y \geq 3x - 5$
$y \geq 1.5x - 2.5$

$-x + 5y > 1$
$5y > x + 1$
$y > 0.2x + 0.2$

These two linear inequalities can be plotted separately on the same graph. Recall that the boundary line of the solution set is found by replacing the inequality symbol ($\geq$ or $>$, in this case) with an equality. If the inequality is absolute ($>$ or $<$), a dashed line is used, since the points on the line do not satisfy the inequality. Otherwise, a solid line is used. The appropriate region can then be shaded.

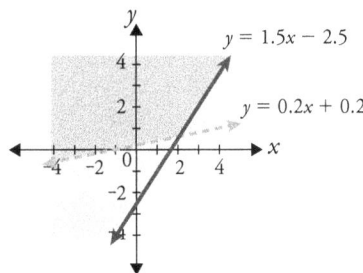

The darkest region is the set of solutions that satisfies both inequalities. Thus, Option A is correct.

(Easy) (Skill 6.7)

32. **Solve for x: $7 - 5x = 7x - 11 - 3x$.**

    A. -2

    B. 2

    C. $-1\frac{1}{2}$

    D. $3\frac{1}{4}$

Answer: B. 2

First add $5x$ to both sides to get all the x terms on one side. Then $7 = 7x - 11 - 3x + 5x$. Combine all the x terms: $7 = 9x - 11$. Add 11 to both sides to get $18 = 9x$. Dividing both sides by 9, $x = 2$.

(Easy) (Skill 7.1)

33. **Which of the following is equivalent to $\sqrt[b]{x^a}$?**

    A. $x^{\frac{a}{b}}$

    B. $x^{\frac{b}{a}}$

    C. $a^{\frac{x}{b}}$

    D. $b^{\frac{x}{a}}$

Answer: A. $x^{\frac{a}{b}}$

The bth root, expressed in the form $\sqrt[b]{\,}$, can also be written as an exponential, $\frac{1}{b}$. Writing the expression in this form, $(x^a)^{\frac{1}{b}}$, and then multiplying exponents, yields $x^{\frac{a}{b}}$.

(Average) (Skill 7.4)

34. **The function shown in the graph below is:**

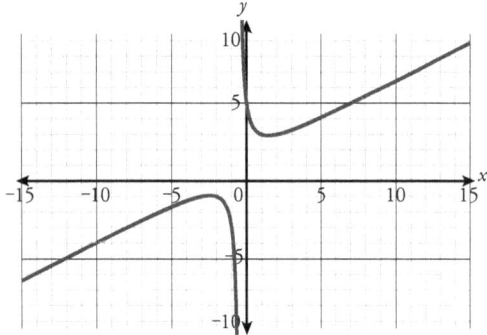

A. $\dfrac{x^2 + 3x + 5}{2x^3 + 1}$

B. $\dfrac{3x + 5}{2x + 1}$

C. $\dfrac{x^2 + 3x + 5}{2x - 1}$

D. $\dfrac{x^2 + 3x + 5}{2x + 1}$

Answer: D. $\dfrac{x^2 + 3x + 5}{2x + 1}$

Since the graph has a slant asymptote, the degree of the polynomial in the numerator must be greater than the degree of the polynomial in the denominator. This eliminates options A and B. Examining the denominators, we see that Option C has a vertical asymptote at $x = \frac{1}{2}$ and Option D has a vertical asymptote at $x = -\frac{1}{2}$. Clearly, the graph is consistent with Option D.

(Rigorous) (Skill 7.6)

35. **Which of the following is a factor of $6 + 48m^3$?**

A. $(1 + 2m)$

B. $(1 - 8m)$

C. $(1 + m - 2m)$

D. $(1 - m + 2m)$

Answer: A. $(1 + 2m)$

Removing the common factor of 6 and then factoring the sum of two cubes yields $6 + 48m^3 = 6(1 + 8m^3) = 6(1 + 2m)(1^2 - 2m + (2m)^2)$.

(Rigorous) (Skill 7.6)

36. **Which expression is equal to $x^4 + 2x^3 - 16x^2 - 2x + 15$ divided by $x + 5$?**

A. $4x^3 + 6x^2 - 32x - 2$

B. $x^3 - 15x^2 - 5x + 15$

C. $x^3 - 3x^2 - x + 3$

D. $5x^3 + 10x^2 - 80x + 75$

Answer: C. $x^3 - 3x^2 - x + 3$

The most direct approach to solving this problem is the use of synthetic division. We can set up the synthetic division as shown below. Inside the division bar, we place the coefficients of the polynomial that we are dividing, and outside the division bar, we write the solution ($x = -5$) corresponding to the factor $x + 5$.

$-5 \,|\; 1 \quad 2 \quad -16 \quad -2 \quad 15$

Next, we start by carrying the first coefficient down to the bottom, then we begin performing the algorithm for synthetic division. The first step is shown below, followed by the final result.

```
-5 | 1   2   -16   -2   15
   |
   ‾‾‾‾‾‾‾‾‾‾‾‾‾‾‾‾‾‾‾‾‾‾‾
     1
```

```
-5 | 1   2   -16   -2   15
   |    -5   15    5   -15
   ‾‾‾‾‾‾‾‾‾‾‾‾‾‾‾‾‾‾‾‾‾‾‾
     1  -3   -1    3    0
```

We can now write the resulting polynomial, which is the solution to the problem: $x^3 - 3x^2 - x + 3$. Of course, an alternative (but tedious) approach to solving this problem is to multiply $x + 5$ by each potential answer to see which product is equal to the original polynomial given in the problem.

(Rigorous) (Skill 8.1)

37. **Which of the following is the algebraic equivalent of the function given below in tabular form?**

x	y
-2	$\frac{1}{8}$
-1	$\frac{1}{2}$
0	2
1	8
2	32

    A. $y = \frac{3}{8}x + 2$

    B. $y = 2(4^x)$

    C. $y = x^2 - \frac{31}{8}$

    D. $y = 4^x$

    Answer: B. $y = 2(4^x)$

Examining the numbers in the table, we see that for a constant change in x, y changes by a constant ratio of 4. This indicates that the function is exponential and the solution is either B or D. For $x = 0, y = 2$. This is consistent with Option B.

(Rigorous) (Skill 8.3)

38. **Solve $\ln x + \ln x^2 + \ln x^3 = 3$.**

    A. $e^{0.5}$

    B. $3^{\frac{1}{6}}$

    C. e^2

    D. 3^6

    Answer: A. $e^{0.5}$

    $\ln x + \ln x^2 + \ln x^3 = 3 \Rightarrow \ln(x \cdot x^2 \cdot x^3)$
    $= 3 \Rightarrow \ln x^6 = 3 \Rightarrow 6 \ln x = 3 \Rightarrow \ln x$
    $= 0.5 \Rightarrow x = e^{0.5}$

(Rigorous) (Skill 8.5)

39. A population P of bacteria doubles in number every hour. Which of the following functions of t in hours best represents the number of bacteria in the population?

   A. P^t
   B. $P(2^t)$
   C. Pt^2
   D. Pe^t

Answer: B. $P(2^t)$

One approach to this problem is to consider some simple numbers. Assume, for instance, that the initial population (time $t = 0$ hours) includes two bacteria. The population at time t is then the following:

t (hours)	P
1	4
2	8
3	16
4	32
5	64
6	128

At this point, you can either attempt to derive an appropriate function or test each function listed in the possible options for the problem. Only Option B yields the numbers in the table; thus, $P(2^t)$ is the correct answer.

(Rigorous) (Skill 8.6)

40. The acidity or alkalinity of a substance is measured using the logarithmic pH scale, where the pH of a substance is given by the equation $pH = -\log_{10}[H^+]$, where $[H^+]$ is the hydrogen ion concentration in moles per liter. If the pH of a substance is 5.5, what is its hydrogen ion concentration in moles per liter?

   A. 3.16×10^{-6}
   B. 4.08×10^{-3}
   C. 3.16×10^{6}
   D. 4.08×10^{3}

Answer: A. 3.16×10^{-6}

$5.5 = -\log_{10}[H^+] \Rightarrow \log_{10}[H^+] = -5.5 \Rightarrow H^+ = 10^{-5.5} = 3.16 \times 10^{-6}$

(Easy) (Skill 9.5)

41. Which of the following is a Pythagorean identity?

   A. $\sin^2 \theta - \cos^2 \theta = 1$
   B. $\sin^2 \theta + \cos^2 \theta = 1$
   C. $\cos^2 \theta - \sin^2 \theta = 1$
   D. $\cos^2 \theta + \tan^2 \theta = 1$

Answer: B. $\sin^2 \theta + \cos^2 \theta = 1$

The Pythagorean identity $\sin^2 \theta + \cos^2 \theta = 1$ is derived from the definitions of the sine and cosine functions and the Pythagorean theorem of geometry.

(Easy) (Skill 9.5)

42. The cosine function is equivalent to:

   A. $\dfrac{1}{\text{sine}}$

   B. $\dfrac{1}{\text{tangent}}$

   C. $\dfrac{\text{sine}}{\text{tangent}}$

   D. $\dfrac{\text{cotangent}}{\text{sine}}$

Answer: C. $\dfrac{\text{sine}}{\text{tangent}}$

The cosine function is clearly not the reciprocal of the sine or tangent functions. Simplify options C and D to determine the correct answer. For instance:

$\dfrac{\text{sine}}{\text{tangent}} = (\text{sine})(\text{cotangent}) = \text{sine}\left(\dfrac{\text{cosine}}{\text{sine}}\right)$
$= \text{cosine}$

Thus, Option C is correct.

(Rigorous) (Skill 9.6)

43. Determine the measure of the angle α in the triangle below.

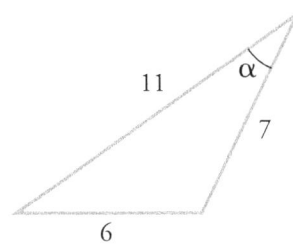

   A. 15.3°

   B. 18°

   C. 29.5°

   D. 45°

Answer: C. 29.5°

We can use the law of cosines to solve this problem. The lengths a, b, and c of a triangle can be used in the formula below to solve for angle C, which is the angle opposite the side with length c.

$c^2 = a^2 + b^2 - 2ab \cos C$

In this case, a and b are 11 and 7 units, and c is 6 units. The angle α opposite side c corresponds to angle C in the formula.

$6^2 = 11^2 + 7^2 - 2(11)(7) \cos \alpha$

$36 = 121 + 49 - 154 \cos \alpha =$
$170 - 154 \cos \alpha$

$154 \cos \alpha = 134$

$\cos \alpha = \dfrac{134}{154} \approx 0.870$

$\alpha = \arccos 0.870 \approx 29.5°$

Thus, angle α is approximately 29.5°.

(Easy) (Skill 10.1)

44. L'Hopital's rule provides a method to evaluate which of the following?

   A. Limit of a function

   B. Derivative of a function

   C. Sum of an arithmetic series

   D. Sum of a geometric series

Answer: A. Limit of a function

L'Hopital's rule is used to find the limit of a function by taking the derivatives of the numerator and denominator. Since the primary purpose of the rule is to find the limit, A is the correct answer.

(Rigorous) (Skill 10.1)

45. Find the following limit: $\lim_{x \to 2} \frac{x^2 - 4}{x - 2}$.

   A. 0
   B. Infinity
   C. 2
   D. 4

Answer: D. 4

Factor the numerator and cancel the common factor to get the limit.

$\lim_{x \to 2} \frac{x^2 - 4}{x - 2} = \lim_{x \to 2} \frac{(x - 2)(x + 2)}{(x - 2)} =$
$\lim_{x \to 2} (x + 2) = 4$

(Rigorous) (Skill 10.3)

46. What is the maximum value of the function $f(x) = -3x^2 - 5$?

   A. -5
   B. -3
   C. 1
   D. 5

Answer: A. -5

First, consider the graph of this function, which is shown below.

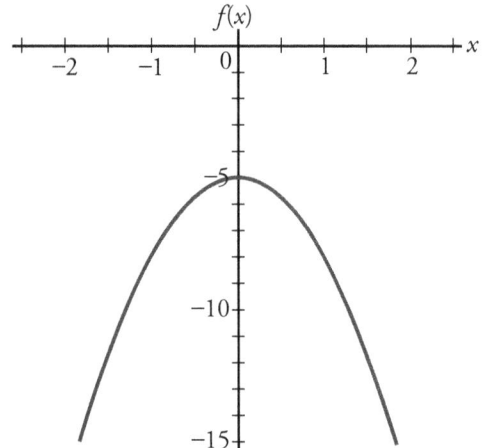

Obviously, the function has a single maximum value. To find the maximum value, first determine the location of the critical points. The critical points correspond to locations where the slope of the function is zero; to find these points, set the first derivative of the function equal to zero, and solve for the variable.

$f'(x) = \frac{d}{dx}(-3x^2 - 5) = -6x$
$-6x = 0$
$x = 0$

Now, to find the maximum value, substitute $x = 0$ into the function $f(x)$.

$f(0) = -3(0)^2 - 5 = -5$

(Rigorous) (Skill 10.3)

47. Find the absolute maximum obtained by the function $y = 2x^2 + 3x$ on the interval $x = 0$ to $x = 3$.

   A. $-\frac{3}{4}$
   B. $-\frac{4}{3}$
   C. 0
   D. 27

Answer: D. 27

Find the critical point at $x = -.75$ by setting the first derivative of the function to zero as performed in question 46: $\frac{d}{dx}(2x^2 + 3x) = 4x + 3 = 0; \Rightarrow 4x = -3; x = -0.75$.

Since the critical point is not in the interval from $x = 0$ to $x = 3$, simply find the values of the function at the endpoints. The endpoints are $x = 0$, $y = 0$, and $x = 3$, $y = 27$. Therefore, 27 is the absolute maximum on the given interval.

ANSWERS WITH RATIONALES

(Rigorous) (Skill 10.4)

48. Find the antiderivative for $4x^3 - 2x + 6 = y$.

    A. $x^4 - x^2 + 6x + C$
    B. $x^4 - \frac{2}{3}x^3 + 6x + C$
    C. $12x^2 - 2 + C$
    D. $\frac{4}{3}x^4 - x^2 + 6x + C$

Answer: A. $x^4 - x^2 + 6x + C$

Use the rule for polynomial integration: given ax^n, the antiderivative is $\frac{ax^{n+1}}{n+1}$. Apply this rule to each term in the polynomial to get the result in Option A.

(Rigorous) (Skill 10.5)

49. The radius of a spherical balloon is increasing at a rate of 2 feet per minute. What is the rate of increase of the volume when the radius is 4 feet?

    A. 4 feet³/minute
    B. 32π feet³/minute
    C. 85.3π feet³/minute
    D. 128π feet³/minute

Answer: D. 128π feet³/minute

Note that the volume V of a sphere in terms of its radius r is the following:

$$V = \frac{4}{3}\pi r^3$$

We want to calculate the rate of change of the volume with respect to time $\left(\frac{dV}{dt}\right)$ in terms of the rate of change of the radius with respect to time $\left(\frac{dr}{dt}\right)$. First, use the chain rule to rewrite the expression for the rate of change of the volume.

$$\frac{dV}{dt} = \frac{dV}{dr}\frac{dr}{dt}$$

Now, calculate the derivative of the volume with respect to the radius.

$$\frac{dV}{dr} = 4\pi r^2$$

Then, $\frac{dV}{dt} = 4\pi r^2 \frac{dr}{dt} = 4\pi r^2 \left(2 \frac{\text{feet}}{\text{minute}}\right)$

$= 8\pi r^2 \frac{\text{feet}}{\text{minute}}$

When the radius is 4 feet, the rate of change of the volume is as follows:

$$\frac{dV}{dt} = 8\pi(4 \text{ feet})^2 \frac{\text{feet}}{\text{minute}} = 128\pi \frac{\text{feet}^3}{\text{minute}}$$

Thus, the rate of change of the volume when the radius is 4 feet is 128π cubic feet per minute.

(Rigorous) (Skill 11.1)

50. Given that M is a mass, V is a velocity, A is an acceleration, and T is a time, what type of unit corresponds to the overall expression $\frac{AMT}{V}$?

    A. Mass
    B. Time
    C. Velocity
    D. Acceleration

Answer: A. Mass

Use unit analysis to find the simplest expression for the units associated with the expression. Choose any unit system: for example, the metric system.

$$\frac{AMT}{V} \sim \frac{\left(\frac{m}{s^2}\right)(kg)(s)}{\left(\frac{m}{s}\right)}$$

Simplify the units in the expression.

$$\frac{AMT}{V} \sim \frac{\left(\frac{m}{s}\right)(kg)}{\left(\frac{m}{s}\right)} = kg$$

Kilograms are a unit of mass, and thus the correct answer is A.

(Average) (Skill 11.1)

51. The term "cubic feet" indicates which kind of measurement?

    A. Volume
    B. Mass
    C. Length
    D. Distance

    Answer: A. Volume

    The word "cubic" indicates that this is a term describing volume.

(Easy) (Skill 11.1)

52. Which unit of measurement would be the most appropriate for characterizing the weight of a dime?

    A. Gram
    B. Kilogram
    C. Pound
    D. Ton

    Answer: A. Gram

    A dime is fairly small and obviously doesn't weigh close to a pound. Thus, neither pound nor kilogram nor ton is an appropriate measurement for a dime.

(Rigorous) (Skill 11.3)

53. When the side of a regular hexagon is doubled, its area increases by a factor of:

    A. 2
    B. 4
    C. $\frac{3}{4}$
    D. $3\sqrt{3}$

    Answer: B. 4

    A regular hexagon of side a is made up of 6 equilateral triangles of side a. The area of each equilateral triangle = $\frac{1}{2} \times a \times \frac{\sqrt{3}a}{2} = \frac{\sqrt{3}a^2}{4}$.

    The area of the hexagon = $\frac{\sqrt{3}a^2}{4} \times 6 = \frac{3\sqrt{3}a^2}{2}$.

    So if the side is increased from a to $2a$, the new area will be 4 times the original area.

    This question can be answered even without working out the actual area of the hexagon. Since a is the only length dimension in the picture, it is sort of intuitively obvious that the area of the hexagon will be some number times a^2. So doubling the length of the side will increase the area by a factor of 4.

(Average) (Skill 11.4)

54. An employee of a security firm is standing on a 10-foot ladder and placing spikes on top of a fence. If the top of the ladder touches the top of the fence and the bottom of the ladder is 4 feet away from the bottom of the fence, how high is the fence?

    A. 6 ft.
    B. 14 ft.
    C. $2\sqrt{21}$ ft.
    D. $2\sqrt{29}$ ft.

    Answer: C. $2\sqrt{21}$ ft.

    The ladder, fence, and ground form a right triangle with the ladder as the hypotenuse. If the height of the fence is h, using the Pythagorean theorem, we can write $10^2 = 4^2 + h^2 \Rightarrow h^2 = 100 - 16 = 84 \Rightarrow h = \sqrt{84} = 2\sqrt{21}$.

(Rigorous) (Skill 12.1)

55. **Which of the following is *not* true of an axiomatic system?**

    A. The theorems are deduced from axioms

    B. It contains both defined and undefined terms

    C. Some axiomatic systems do not contain undefined terms

    D. All parts of an axiomatic system are consistent with each other

Answer: C. Some axiomatic systems do not contain undefined terms

All axiomatic systems must consist of some undefined terms since any term that is defined uses other terms for the purpose of definition. If these terms in turn are defined, then there must be other new terms used to define them and so on. This chain of definition cannot continue ad infinitum. At some point there must be one or more terms that are undefined and simply accepted as self-evident.

(Rigorous) (Skill 12.2)

56. **In the figure shown below, angle $AOB = 30°$, angle $FOE = (3x − 10)°$, and angle $DOC = x°$. What is the value of x?**

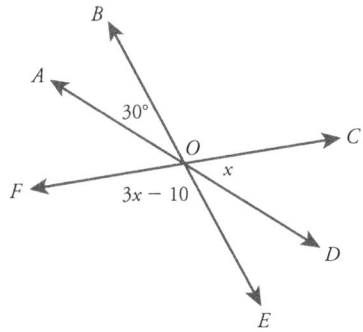

A. 30°

B. 40°

C. 60°

D. 110°

Answer: B. 40°

Angle $EOD = 30°$ since EOD and AOB are vertical angles. Angles FOE, EOD, and DOC add up to 180° since FOC is a straight line. So $3x − 10 + 30 + x = 180 \Rightarrow 4x + 20 = 180 \Rightarrow 4x = 160 \Rightarrow x = 40$.

(Average) (Skill 12.3)

57. **In the figure below, angles x and y are equal. From this we can conclude that:**

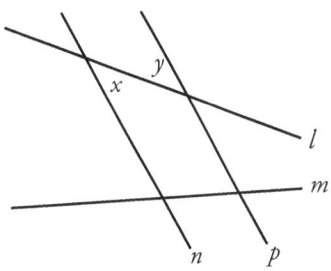

A. Lines l and m are parallel

B. Lines n and p are parallel

C. Lines m and p are perpendicular

D. Lines n and l are perpendicular

Answer: B. Lines n and p are parallel

Angles x and y are alternate interior angles created by the transversal l that cuts lines n and p. Since the alternate interior angles are equal, n and p are parallel.

(Average) (Skill 12.4)

58. *ABC* and *DEF* are similar triangles where $\angle A = \angle D$, $\angle B = \angle E$, $\angle C = \angle F$, $AB = 5$ cm, $DE = 7.5$ cm, and $BC = 6$ cm. What is the length of *EF*?

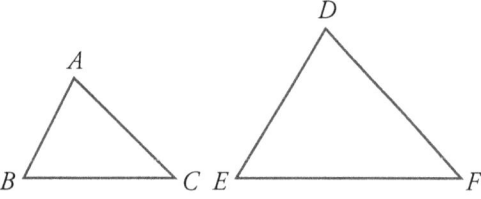

A. 9 cm

B. 4 cm

C. 6.25 cm

D. 8.5 cm

Answer: A. 9 cm

Since the triangles *ABC* and *DEF* are similar, their sides are proportional. So $\frac{AB}{DE} = \frac{AC}{DF} = \frac{BC}{EF} \Rightarrow \frac{5}{7.5} = \frac{6}{EF} \Rightarrow EF = \frac{6 \times 7.5}{5} = 9$.

(Rigorous) (Skill 13.1)

59. Choose the correct statement concerning the median and altitude in a triangle.

A. The median and altitude of a triangle may be the same segment

B. The median and altitude of a triangle are always different segments

C. The median and altitude of a right triangle are always the same segment

D. The median and altitude of an isosceles triangle are always the same segment

Answer: A. The median and altitude of a triangle may be the same segment

The most one can say with certainty is that the median (segment drawn to the midpoint of the opposite side) and the altitude (segment drawn perpendicular to the opposite side) of a triangle *may* coincide, but they more often do not. In an isosceles triangle, the median and the altitude to the *base* are the same segment.

(Average) (Skill 13.1)

60. Which of the following is *not* true? An equilateral triangle:

A. Has three equal sides

B. Has three equal angles

C. Has three acute angles

D. Has three obtuse angles

Answer: D. Has three obtuse angles

An equilateral triangle, by definition, has three equal sides. So the three angles are equal as well and each is an acute angle equal to 60°.

(Rigorous) (Skill 13.4)

61. Given a 30-by-60-meter garden with a circular fountain with a 5-meter radius, calculate the area of the portion of the garden *not* occupied by the fountain.

A. 1,721 m²

B. 1,879 m²

C. 2,585 m²

D. 1,015 m²

Answer: A. 1,721 m²

Find the area of the garden and then subtract the area of the fountain: $30(60) - \pi(5)^2$ or approximately 1,721 square meters.

ANSWERS WITH RATIONALES

(Easy) (Skill 13.5)

62. The cross-section of a three-dimensional figure is circular in shape. The figure could be a:

    I. Sphere
    II. Cylinder
    III. Cone
    IV. Rectangular prism

    A. I only
    B. I and II
    C. I, II, and III
    D. I, II, III, and IV

    Answer: C. I, II, and III

    Since a rectangular prism is made up of straight edges, there is no way one can cut it to produce a circular cross-section. A sphere will produce a circular cross-section when cut in any direction. A cylinder and cone will produce a circular cross-section when cut by a plane parallel to the base.

(Rigorous) (Skill 14.4)

63. A figure placed in quadrant II of the *x-y* coordinate plane is rotated 90° counter-clockwise about the origin in the *x-y* plane and then reflected in the *x*-axis. The final position of the figure is in:

    A. Quadrant I
    B. Quadrant II
    C. Quadrant III
    D. Quadrant IV

    Answer: B. Quadrant II

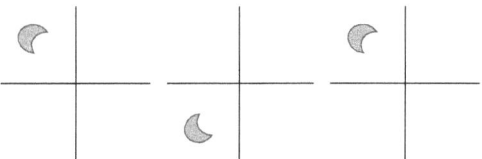

Original position   After rotation   After reflection

(Rigorous) (Skill 14.5)

64. Two points have coordinates (3, -4, 1) and (6, 2, -7). What is the distance between these points?

    A. 7 units
    B. 10.4 units
    C. 13.5 units
    D. 15 units

    Answer: B. 10.4 units

    The locations of these points are expressed using three-dimensional coordinates. The distance d can be calculated using the distance formula as follows:

    $$\sqrt{(x_1 - x_2)^2 + (y_1 - y_2)^2 + (z_1 - z_2)^2} =$$
    $$\sqrt{(3 - 6)^2 + (-4 - 2)^2 + (1 + 7)^2}$$
    $$\sqrt{(-3)^2 + (-6)^2 + (8)^2} =$$
    $$\sqrt{9 + 36 + 64} = \sqrt{109} \approx 10.4.$$

(Rigorous) (Skill 14.6)

65. What are the foci of the ellipse $16(y-3)^2 = 16 - (x-2)^2$?

    A. $(2\pm 4, 3)$
    B. $(-2\pm\sqrt{15}, -3)$
    C. $(2\pm\sqrt{15}, 3)$
    D. $(2, 3\pm\sqrt{15})$

Answer: C. $(2\pm\sqrt{15}, 3)$

We can start by attempting to express the equation in standard form for an ellipse:

$$\frac{(x-h)^2}{a^2} + \frac{(y-k)^2}{b^2} = 1$$

Here, (h, k) is the center of the ellipse, and a and b are half the axis lengths. (Depending on the particular values, a or b can be half of the minor or major axis.)

$$16(y-3)^2 = 16 - (x-2)^2$$
$$(y-3)^2 = 1 - \frac{(x-2)^2}{16}$$
$$\frac{(x-2)^2}{16} + \frac{(y-3)^2}{1} = 1$$

On the basis of comparison with the standard form, we can quickly see that the center of the ellipse is located at $(2, 3)$. The major axis is parallel to the x-axis, and it has a half-length of 4 units (the square root of 16). We know that the foci are located on the major axis. Their locations are $(h\pm c, k)$, where

$$c = \sqrt{a^2 - b^2}.$$

In this case,

$$c = \sqrt{16 - 1} = \sqrt{15}.$$

The foci are then located at $(2\pm\sqrt{15}, 3)$.

(Rigorous) (Skill 14.7)

66. Which of the following best describes the translation matrix below for arbitrary points (x_1, y_1)?

$$\begin{pmatrix} 1 & 0 \\ 0 & -1 \end{pmatrix} \begin{pmatrix} x_1 \\ y_1 \end{pmatrix} = \begin{pmatrix} x_2 \\ y_2 \end{pmatrix}$$

    A. Rotation
    B. Translation
    C. Reflection
    D. Dilation

Answer: C. Reflection

Perform the matrix multiplication to see what happens to the point (x_1, y_1).

$$\begin{pmatrix} 1 & 0 \\ 0 & -1 \end{pmatrix} \begin{pmatrix} x_1 \\ y_1 \end{pmatrix} = \begin{pmatrix} x_1 \\ -y_1 \end{pmatrix}$$

Notice, then, that the result is a corresponding point on the opposite side of the x-axis. Thus, this translation matrix reflects points across the x-axis.

(Rigorous) (Skill 14.8)

67. Determine the rectangular coordinates of the point with polar coordinates $(5, 60°)$.

    A. $(0.5, 0.87)$
    B. $(-0.5, 0.87)$
    C. $(2.5, 4.33)$
    D. $(25, 150°)$

Answer: C. $(2.5, 4.33)$

Given the polar point $(r, \theta) = (5, 60)$, the rectangular coordinates can be found as follows: $(x, y) = (r\cos\theta, r\sin\theta) = (5\cos 60, 5\sin 60) = (2.5, 4.33)$.

ANSWERS WITH RATIONALES

(Average) (Skill 15.2)

68. Which of the following types of graphs would *not* be used to record the eye color of the students in the class?

    A. Bar graph
    B. Line graph
    C. Pictograph
    D. Circle graph

Answer: B. Line graph

In this activity, a line graph would not be used because it typically shows change over time. Any of the other types of graphs could be used to show the number or percentage of students with brown eyes, blue eyes, and so on.

(Easy) (Skill 15.2)

69. What conclusion can be drawn from the graph below?

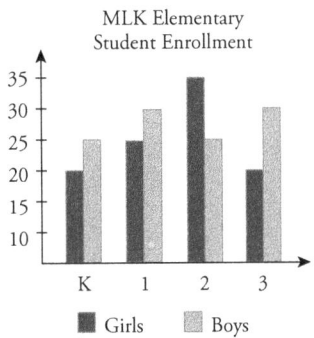

A. The number of students in first grade exceeds the number in second grade
B. There are more boys than girls in the entire school
C. There are more girls than boys in the first grade
D. Third grade has the largest number of students

Answer: B. There are more boys than girls in the entire school

In kindergarten, first grade, and third grade, there are more boys than girls. The number of extra girls in grade two is more than compensated by the extra boys in all the other grades put together.

(Easy) (Skill 15.2)

70. The pie chart below shows sales at an automobile dealership for the first four months of a year. What percentage of the vehicles were sold in April?

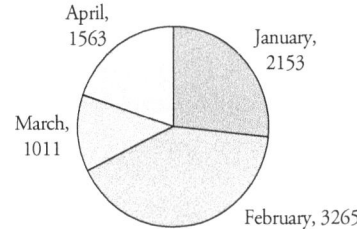

A. More than 50%
B. Less than 25%
C. Between 25% and 50%
D. None

Answer: B. Less than 25%

It is clear from the chart that the April segment covers less than a quarter of the pie.

PRETEST

(Easy) (Skill 15.3)

71. **Which word best describes a set of measured values that are all very similar but deviate significantly from the expected result?**

    A. Perfect

    B. Precise

    C. Accurate

    D. Appropriate

Answer: B. Precise

A set of measurements that are close to the same value is *precise*. Measurements that are close to the actual (or expected) value are *accurate*. In this case, the set of measurements described in the question is best summarized as precise.

(Average) (Skill 15.3)

72. **An archer's paper target shows the hits illustrated below. Which term best describes the archer's shooting in this case?**

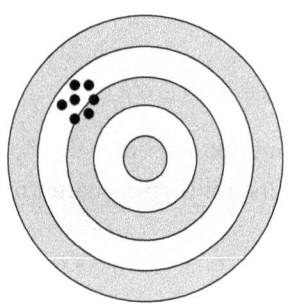

    A. Accurate

    B. Precise

    C. Exact

    D. On target

Answer: B. Precise

The archer shows *precision* in his shooting, in that the hits are tightly grouped in a small area. Because that group is off center, however, the archer is not *accurate*. The terms "exact" and "on target" do not apply in this case.

(Easy) (Skill 15.4)

73. **Compute the median for the following data set:**

    {12, 19, 13, 16, 17, 14}

    A. 14.5

    B. 15.17

    C. 15

    D. 16

Answer: C. 15

Arrange the data in ascending order: 12, 13, 14, 16, 17, 19. The median is the middle value in a list with an odd number of entries. When there is an even number of entries, the median is the mean of the two center entries. Here the average of 14 and 16 is 15.

(Rigorous) (Skill 15.4)

74. **What is the standard deviation of the following sample?**

    {1.46, 1.55, 1.55, 1.57, 1.89, 2.01, 2.09}

    A. 0.010

    B. 0.066

    C. 0.26

    D. 1.73

Answer: C. 0.26

Notice first that the problem stated that the data set is a *sample*. Thus, we need to use sample statistics (as will be discussed further). To start, we must calculate the mean $\bar{x}$ of the data.

$$\bar{x} = \frac{1.46 + 1.55 + 1.55 + 1.57 + 1.89 + 2.01 + 2.09}{7}$$
$$\approx 1.73$$

The standard deviation is the square root of the sample variance, s^2, which is given below.

$$s^2 = \frac{1}{n-1}\sum_i (x_i - \bar{x})^2$$
$$s^2 = \frac{1}{6}[(1.46 - 1.73)^2 + (1.55 - 1.73)^2 + \cdots + (2.09 - 1.73)^2]$$
$$s^2 = \frac{1}{6}[0.073 + 0.032 + \cdots + 0.130] \approx 0.066$$
$$s = \sqrt{s^2} \approx \sqrt{0.066} \approx 0.26$$

The standard deviation s is then 0.26.

(Rigorous) (Skill 15.4)

75. **Which measure of central tendency best characterizes the data set below?**

Value	Frequency
1	2
2	5
3	7
4	3
5	2
6	1
7	1

A. Mean

B. Median

C. Both the mean and median are the same

D. None of the above

Answer: A. Mean

By plotting the data on a bar graph or histogram, we can visualize the shape of the data distribution.

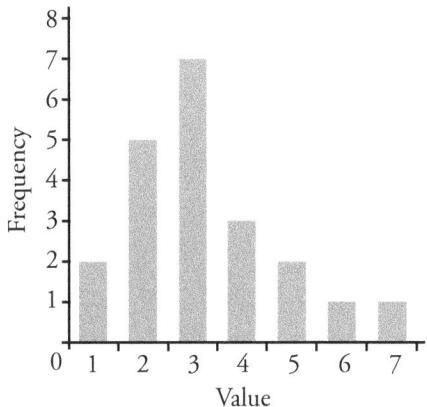

Because the distribution is skewed rather than symmetric, it is not immediately clear that the mean or median is the better choice in this situation. The median is 4 (the data set contains a total of 21 values). We can calculate the mean using a weighted average as shown below.

$$\bar{x} = \frac{1 \cdot 2 + 2 \cdot 5 + 3 \cdot 7 + \cdots + 7 \cdot 1}{2 + 5 + 7 + \cdots + 1} = \frac{68}{21} \approx 3.24$$

The mean in this case is a little closer to the peak. Given the shape of the distribution, the mean is therefore a better choice than the median.

(Rigorous) (Skill 16.2)

76. **How many different five-card hands containing three aces and two kings can be drawn from a standard 52-card deck?**

    A. 6
    B. 16
    C. 24
    D. 2,598,960

    Answer: C. 24

    A standard 52-card deck contains four kings and four aces. The number of five-card hands containing three aces and two kings can be found as the product of the number of combinations of three aces and the number of combinations of two kings. The solution N is the following, where $\binom{n}{k}$ is the number of combinations of n objects taken k at a time.

    $$N = \binom{4}{3} \cdot \binom{4}{2} = 4 \cdot 6 = 24$$

    Thus, 24 possible five-card hands have three aces and two kings.

(Average) (Skill 16.3)

77. **What is the probability that a roll of a six-sided die yields an outcome that is even or greater than three?**

    A. $\frac{3}{6}$
    B. $\frac{4}{6}$
    C. $\frac{5}{6}$
    D. 1

    Answer: B. $\frac{4}{6}$

    The sample space for a single roll of a six-sided die is 1, 2, 3, 4, 5, 6. The outcomes that satisfy the condition of being even or greater than three are 2, 4, 5, 6. Thus, four out of a total of six possible outcomes result in a "successful" trial. The corresponding probability is then $\frac{4}{6} = \frac{2}{3}$, or approximately 0.67.

(Easy) (Skill 16.3)

78. **On the throw of a six-sided die, what is the probability that you will roll a number less than three?**

    A. $\frac{1}{2}$
    B. $\frac{1}{6}$
    C. $\frac{1}{3}$
    D. $\frac{2}{3}$

    Answer: C. $\frac{1}{3}$

    To find the probability, divide the number of acceptable outcomes by the total number of possible outcomes. The acceptable outcomes are 1 and 2, so there are two of them. The total number of possible outcomes is 6. So the probability of rolling a number less than 3 is $\frac{2}{6}$, which reduces to $\frac{1}{3}$.

(Rigorous) (Skill 16.4)

79. **Three identical green chairs and four identical red chairs are randomly arranged in a single row. What is the probability that no chair will be placed next to one of the same color?**

    A. $\frac{1}{7}$
    B. $\frac{1}{35}$
    C. $\frac{3}{7}$
    D. $\frac{3}{35}$

    Answer: B. $\frac{1}{35}$

The number of ways 7 objects can be arranged in a row = 7!

Since 3 of the chairs are identical and so are the remaining 4, the number of ways 3 green chairs and 4 red chairs can be arranged in a row = $\frac{7!}{3!4!} = \frac{5 \times 6 \times 7}{2 \times 3} = 35$.

Of the 35 possible arrangements, there is only one in which no chair is placed next to one of the same color: GRGRGRG. Hence the probability that no chair is placed next to one of the same color is $\frac{1}{35}$.

(Rigorous) (Skill 16.6)

80. **A baseball team has a 60% chance of winning any particular game in a 7-game series. What is the probability that it will win the series by winning games 6 and 7?**

    A. 8.3%
    B. 36%
    C. 50%
    D. 60%

Answer: A. 8.3%

The team needs to win 4 games to win a 7-game series. Thus, if the team needs to win games 6 and 7 to win the series, it can only win 2 of the first 5 games. There are 10 different ways in which the team can win 2 of the first 5 games (where W represents a win and L represents a loss): WWLLL, WLLLW, WLLWL, WLWLL, LWWLL, LWLWL, LWLLW, LLWLW, LLWWL, and LLLWW. This is also the same as the number of combinations of 5 taken 2 at a time. In each case, the probability that the team will win two games and lose three is the following:

P(2 wins and 3 losses) $= (0.6)^2(0.4)^3 = 0.02304$

Since there are 10 ways this can occur, the probability of 2 wins out of 5 consecutive games is

P(2 wins out of 5 games) $= 10(0.6)^2(0.4)^3 = 0.2304$

The probability of the team winning the last 2 consecutive games is simply 0.6^2, or 0.36. Then, the probability that the team will win the series by winning games 6 and 7 is the following:

P(Series win with wins in games 6 and 7) $= (0.2304)(0.36) = 0.082944 \sim 8.3\%$

(Easy) (Skill 17.1)

81. **In a statistical experiment, a sample is:**

    A. The total set of possible observations
    B. A single observation
    C. A set of observations selected from the population
    D. None of the above

Answer: C. A set of observations selected from the population

The total set of possible observations in a statistical experiment is known as the population. A sample is a set of observations selected from the population. For example, the residents of a city taking part in a survey form a sample. All the residents of the city form the population.

(Average) (Skill 17.4)

82. The height of people in a certain city is a normally distributed random variable. If a person is chosen from the city at random, what is the probability that he or she has a height greater than the mean of the distribution?

    A. 0.25

    B. 0.5

    C. 0.75

    D. Not enough information

Answer: B. 0.5

A normal distribution is symmetric about the mean, as shown below.

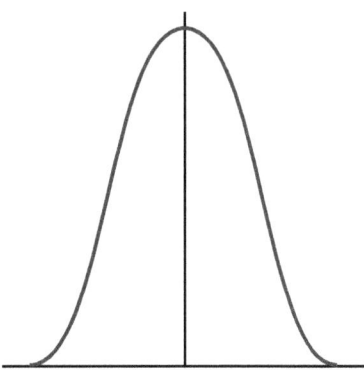

As such, the probability that a particular value is greater than (or less than) the mean is 0.5, since half the probability density is on one side of the mean, and the other half is on the other side.

(Average) (Skill 17.5)

83. Which of the following is the best kind of function for a regression fit of the data shown in the plot below?

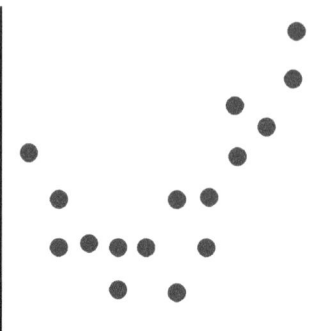

    A. Linear

    B. Quadratic

    C. Exponential

    D. Logarithmic

Answer: B. Quadratic

A function that more or less follows the trend of the data is a good choice. In this case the scattered points appear to clearly make a parabola. Therefore, a quadratic function would be the right kind of function to fit the data.

(Average) (Skill 17.7)

84. **According to the central limit theorem:**

    A. The larger the sample size, the closer the sample mean is to the population mean

    B. The larger the sample size, the closer the correlation coefficient is to 1

    C. As the number of samples increases, the correlation coefficient is closer to 1

    D. As the number of samples increases, the distribution of sample means approaches a normal distribution

Answer: D. As the number of samples increases, the distribution of sample means approaches a normal distribution

The central limit theorem states that as the number of samples increases, the distribution of sample means approaches a normal distribution. Thus, as the number of samples taken increases, the sample mean becomes closer to the population mean.

(Average) (Skill 17.8)

85. Of 75 students surveyed in a school, 50 had perfect attendance for the year. Estimate the fraction of students in the entire school that had perfect attendance using a point estimator from the given sample.

   A. $\frac{2}{3}$
   B. 66%
   C. $\frac{5}{7}$
   D. $\frac{1}{3}$

Answer: A. $\frac{2}{3}$

Assuming that the sample accurately represents the entire student body, the fraction of students with perfect attendance in the sample can be used as a point estimator to estimate the fraction of students in the whole school with perfect attendance. This number $= \frac{50}{75} = \frac{2}{3}$.

(Average) (Skill 18.1)

86. Which of the following are valid methods of mathematical proof?

   I. Show that the conclusion follows necessarily from the premises by going through logical steps, each of which follows from the previous step.

   II. Disprove a statement by providing a single counterexample.

   III. Prove a statement by showing that assuming it to be false leads to a contradiction.

   A. I and II
   B. I and III
   C. II and III
   D. I, II, and III

Answer: D. I, II, and III

Choice I outlines the usual method of direct proof by logically deriving the conclusion from the premises. Choice II is valid because a single counterexample can disprove a statement although any number of examples cannot prove it. For instance, the sighting of a white crow disproves the statement "All crows are black" although one cannot prove the statement by producing any number of black crows. Choice III outlines the method of indirect proof.

(Average) (Skill 18.2)

87. Let x, y, and z represent mathematical statements. Which of the following is a valid conclusion based on the premises given below?

    I. If x, then y
    II. If y, then z

    A. If x, then z
    B. If z, then x
    C. If y, then x
    D. If z, then y

    Answer: A. If x, then z

    "If x, then y" says that if x is true, then y is true. It does not imply that y is true only if x is true. y may be true even if x is not true. Therefore, we cannot conclude that "If y, then x." For the same reason, options B and D are invalid conclusions. However, A is correct since if x is true, then y must be true, and if y is true, then z must be true.

(Average) (Skill 19.1)

88. A student is given the angle measures of two similar triangles ABC and DEF and the lengths of some of the sides. He is asked to find the lengths of the other sides. What would be a good first step in approaching this problem?

    A. Make a list of the steps to be used to solve the problem
    B. Guess the lengths and check if the proportions are correct
    C. Draw a diagram showing the two labeled triangles and side lengths
    D. Try to first find the solution to a simpler problem

    Answer: C. Draw a diagram showing the two labeled triangles and side lengths

    For any geometry problem, drawing a labeled diagram is a crucial first step.

(Rigorous) (Skill 18.6)

89. A student makes temperature measurements outdoors starting at 10 a.m. and ending at 2 p.m. The temperature is 50°F at 10 a.m. and increases by about 1°F every half hour. She sets up a mathematical model to represent her observations. Which of the following is an incorrect use of the model?

    A. The equation $T = 50 + 2h$ is written to represent the temperature between 10 a.m. and 2 p.m.
    B. Using the model, the temperature is estimated to be 52.5°F at 11:15 a.m.
    C. Using the model, the temperature is estimated to be 66°F at 6 p.m.
    D. None of the above

    Answer: C. Using the model, the temperature is estimated to be 66°F at 6 p.m.

    The observations show that the rise in temperature is linear in the relatively narrow time frame of 10 a.m. to 2 p.m. While it is appropriate to use the model to estimate the temperature at another time within that range (e.g., 11:15 a.m.), it is not appropriate to extrapolate the model all the way to 6 p.m., which is far outside the observed range.

ANSWERS WITH RATIONALES

(Average) (Skill 19.1)

90. Students in a classroom are led through an activity in which they fold a sheet of paper in half, fold it again to halve the area, and keep folding it in successive halves as many times as they can. They are usually surprised to discover that the piece of paper gets really small after just a few folds. This exercise is used to represent the mathematical concept of:

    A. Proportional reasoning
    B. Percentage
    C. The area of a rectangle
    D. The exponential function

    Answer: D. The exponential function

    Since the area of the paper decreases by a factor of $\frac{1}{2}$ with each fold, after n folds the area has been reduced by a factor of $\left(\frac{1}{2}\right)^n$. This is an exponential function.

(Average) (Skill 19.3)

91. Which words in a test problem would indicate that an addition operation is needed?

    A. Each
    B. How many
    C. In each group
    D. How many more than

    Answer: B. How many

    Addition operations are indicated by the following words: *total, sum, in all, join, how many.* Subtraction operations are indicated by the following words: *difference, how many more than, how many less than, left.* Multiplication operations are indicated by the following words: *in all, each, of.* Division operations are indicated by the following words: *in each group, per, divide.*

(Rigorous) (Skill 19.4)

92. What is the main purpose of having kindergarten students count by twos?

    A. To hear a rhythm
    B. To recognize patterns in numbers
    C. To practice addition
    D. To become familiar with equations

    Answer: B. To recognize patterns in numbers

    Recognizing patterns in numbers is an early skill for multiplication. It will also help children recognize patterns in word families such as "bit, hit, fit."

(Average) (Skill 19.6)

93. What is the correct mathematical term for the distance from the origin to a point on a graph where a straight line crosses the *x*-axis or *y*-axis?

    A. Cutoff point
    B. Intercept
    C. Slope
    D. Asymptote

    Answer: B. Intercept

    The distance from the origin to a point on a graph where a straight line crosses the *x*-axis or *y*-axis is known as the *x*-intercept or *y*-intercept.

(Easy) (Skill 20.2)

94. The best way to help a visual learner understand a mathematical problem is to:

    A. Draw a diagram to represent the problem
    B. Explain the problem in simple words
    C. Provide manipulatives to model the problem
    D. Allow the student to move around while working on the problem

    Answer: A. Draw a diagram to represent the problem

    Although all the options are valid ways to help a student learn, a visual learner will benefit most from having the information presented visually in the form of a diagram.

(Rigorous) (Skill 20.6)

95. When a student completes the following number sentence, which mathematical concept is being learned?

    $15 - x = 6$

    A. Addition/subtraction and basic algebraic concepts
    B. Counting and addition/subtraction
    C. Counting and basic algebraic concepts
    D. Counting and pattern recognition

    Answer: A. Addition/subtraction and basic algebraic concepts

    Students may use basic addition or subtraction by rearranging the numbers.

    They are also demonstrating the algebraic concept of finding the value of a missing number.

(Rigorous) (Skill 20.6)

96. Students completing an activity with tangrams are learning which mathematical principle?

    A. Basic geometric concepts
    B. Repeating patterns
    C. Counting
    D. Identity property

    Answer: A. Basic geometric concepts

    The students are learning basic geometric concepts (number of sides and types of angles). The tangram picture may or may not be a repeating design. Counting and the identity property (a number plus zero always equals the original number) are not involved.

(Rigorous) (Skill 20.6)

97. Kindergarten students are participating in a calendar time activity. One student adds a straw to the "ones can" to represent that day of school. Which mathematical principle is being reinforced?

    A. Properties of a base ten number system
    B. Sorting
    C. Counting by twos
    D. Even and odd numbers

    Answer: A. Properties of a base ten number system

    As the students group straws into groups of tens to represent the days of school, they are learning the properties of our base ten number system.

(Average) (Skill 20.6)

98. **The purpose of a formative assessment is to:**

    A. Provide parents and school with an intermediate progress report

    B. Assess learning outcomes for a certain time period

    C. Provide feedback to the student and teacher to help the student improve

    D. Test the validity of the assessment method

    Answer: C. Provide feedback to the student and teacher to help the student improve

    As the word "form" indicates, a formative assessment is used to guide the student and provide him or her with an opportunity to improve before a final assessment is made. A summative assessment, by contrast, is a measure of the final outcome of the learning process.

(Average) (Skill 21.2)

99. **An assessment must *not*:**

    A. Be based on material taught in class

    B. Ask students to use mathematical methods familiar to them

    C. Be similar to homework problems

    D. Consist of unfamiliar material to assess how well students can think on their feet

    Answer: D. Consist of unfamiliar material to assess how well students can think on their feet

    Questions on assessments must be consistent with what students have been taught, and they should only be asked to use methods and procedures with which they are familiar.

(Rigorous) (Skill 21.3)

100. **In a geometry assessment, the teacher provides a verbal description of a problem and does not include a diagram. What is the most likely reason for this omission?**

    A. The teacher wishes to test the students' ability to accurately translate the verbal description to a diagram

    B. Creating a diagram would take too much effort

    C. The problem is a test of mathematical terminology

    D. The teacher wishes to raise the difficulty level of the problem

    Answer: A. The teacher wishes to test the students' ability to accurately translate the verbal description to a diagram

    Option C is partly correct because the students will have to understand the terminology to be able to translate it to a visual form. But the main goal of the problem would be to test the students' ability to accurately translate the verbal description to a diagram.

POSTTEST

POSTTEST

(Easy) (Skill 1.1)

1. The digit 3 in the number 129.0035 is in the:

   A. Hundreds place
   B. Hundredths place
   C. Thousands place
   D. Thousandths place

(Average) (Skill 1.3)

2. Which property of real numbers is used in going from Step 1 to Step 2?

   Step 1: $(3a + 4) + {-4} = 12$

   Step 2: $3a + (4 + {-4}) = 12$

   A. Inverse property
   B. Identity property
   C. Associative property
   D. Commutative property

(Average) (Skill 1.4)

3. The distance from the earth to the sun is 90 million miles. Which of the following expresses this number correctly in scientific notation?

   A. 90,000,000
   B. 90×10^6
   C. 9.0×10^6
   D. 9.0×10^7

(Average) (Skill 1.6)

4. Reena ate one-third of all the candy pieces she received when trick-or-treating on Halloween. She gave half the remaining candy to her brother. If six pieces of candy are left over, how many pieces of candy did Reena have in the beginning?

   A. 36
   B. 18
   C. 12
   D. 24

(Rigorous) (Skill 2.2)

5. Which of the following complex numbers have the same modulus?

   $3 + 4i, -5 + 2i, 4 + \sqrt{13}i, \sqrt{5} - 6i$

   A. $3 + 4i$ and $-5 + 2i$
   B. $-5 + 2i$ and $4 + \sqrt{13}i$
   C. $4 + \sqrt{13}i$ and $\sqrt{5} - 6i$
   D. $3 + 4i$ and $\sqrt{5} - 6i$

(Rigorous) (Skill 2.4)

6. Which of the following complex operations is represented in the vector diagram below?

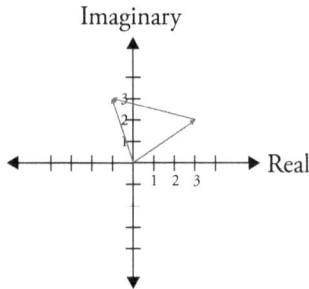

A. $(3 + 2i) + (-4 + i) = -1 + 3i$

B. $(3 + 2i) + (-1 + 3i) = 2 + 5i$

C. $(3 + 2i) \times (-4 + i) = -1 + 3i$

D. $(3 + 2i) + (-4 + i) = 3 - i$

(Rigorous) (Skill 2.5)

7. The complex numbers $1 + 2i$ and $1 - 2i$ are roots of the quadratic equation:

A. $x^2 + 4 = 0$

B. $x^2 - 2x + 5 = 0$

C. $x^2 + 2x + 5 = 0$

D. $x^2 - 2 = 0$

(Easy) (Skill 3.1)

8. Find the GCF of 12, 42, and 78.

A. 2

B. 4

C. 6

D. 12

(Easy) (Skill 3.3)

9. Find the sum of the following matrices:

$$\begin{pmatrix} 6 & 3 \\ 9 & 15 \end{pmatrix} \begin{pmatrix} 4 & 7 \\ 1 & 0 \end{pmatrix}$$

A. $\begin{pmatrix} 10 & 10 \\ 10 & 15 \end{pmatrix}$

B. $\begin{pmatrix} 13 & 7 \\ 9 & 16 \end{pmatrix}$

C. 45

D. $\begin{pmatrix} 20 \\ 25 \end{pmatrix}$

(Easy) (Skill 3.3)

10. The product of two matrices can be found only if:

A. The number of rows in the first matrix is equal to the number of rows in the second matrix

B. The number of columns in the first matrix is equal to the number of columns in the second matrix

C. The number of columns in the first matrix is equal to the number of rows in the second matrix

D. The number of rows in the first matrix is equal to the number of columns in the second matrix

(Easy) (Skill 3.3)

11. Which of the following properties does *not* apply to matrix multiplication?

A. Associativity

B. Commutativity

C. Distributivity

D. All of the above

(Easy) (Skill 3.4)

12. Ron bakes a cake using a recipe that calls for 5 cups of flour and 4 cups of sugar. When he measures out the flour he finds that he only has $4\frac{1}{2}$ cups. How many cups of sugar should he use?

   A. $3\frac{3}{5}$
   B. $3\frac{1}{2}$
   C. 5
   D. $3\frac{4}{5}$

(Rigorous) (Skill 4.1)

13. Which of the following graphs is the next in the sequence of graphs shown below?

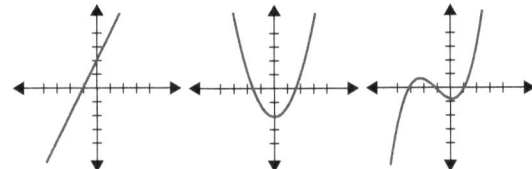

A.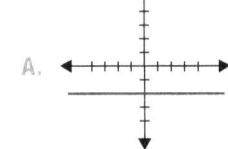

B.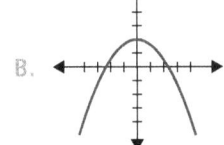

C.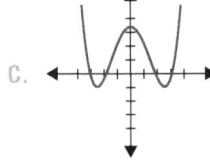

D.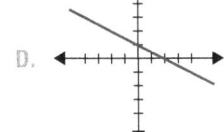

(Average) (Skill 4.3)

14. To prove by mathematical induction that $1^2 + 3^2 + 5^2 + ... + (2N - 1)^2 = N^2$, one must first show that this is true for $N = 1$ and also that:

   A. It is true for $N = 2, 3, 4, 5,$ and 6
   B. It is true for $N = k$ and for $N = k + 1$
   C. If it is true for $N = k$, then it is also true for $N = k + 1$
   D. None of the above

(Average) (Skill 4.4)

15. The sequence given below is:

   $\{\frac{2}{3}, \frac{2}{5}, \frac{6}{25}, \frac{18}{125}, ...\}$

   A. An arithmetic series with common difference $\frac{4}{15}$
   B. An arithmetic series with common ratio $\frac{3}{5}$
   C. A geometric series with common difference $\frac{4}{15}$
   D. A geometric series with common ratio $\frac{3}{5}$

(Average) (Skill 5.1)

16. The list of (x, y) points given below represents:

   $\{(1, 5), (3, 2), (-1, 4), (1, 2), (2, 5)\}$

   A. A relation with domain $\{-1, 1, 2, 3\}$
   B. A function with domain $\{-1, 1, 2, 3\}$
   C. A relation with domain $\{2, 4, 5\}$
   D. A function with domain $\{2, 4, 5\}$

(Rigorous) (Skill 5.2)

17. What is the domain of the function $\frac{x+1}{x^2+2x-3}$?

    A. $x \neq -3, 1$
    B. $x \neq 3, -1$
    C. $x \neq -\frac{3}{2}$
    D. All values of x

(Rigorous) (Skill 5.5)

18. If a transformation of the form $f(x - k) + m$, where k and m are positive numbers, is applied to a function $f(x)$, the graph of the function will be displaced:

    A. Upward and toward the right
    B. Upward and toward the left
    C. Downward and toward the right
    D. Downward and toward the left

(Rigorous) (Skill 5.6)

19. Which of the following functions does *not* have an inverse?

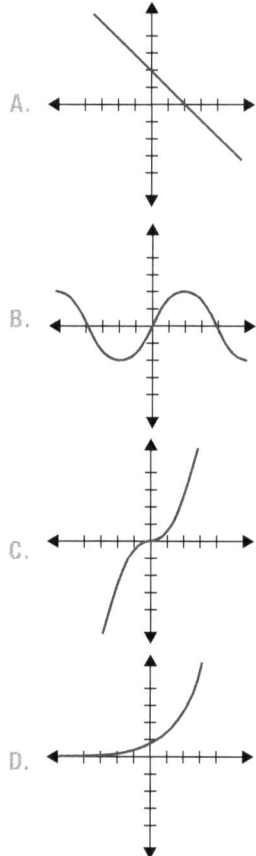

(Rigorous) (Skill 5.7)

20. Which of the following functions share the same graphical representation?

    I. $\ln x + \ln x^3$
    II. $4 \ln x$
    III. $\ln(e^{4 \ln x})$

    A. I and II
    B. I and III
    C. II and III
    D. I, II, and III

(Rigorous) (Skill 6.1)

21. Debbie finances a house with a $10,000 down payment and a monthly payment of $700. The total payment y made after x months is expressed as a linear function $y = f(x)$ that is plotted on a coordinate plane. Which of the following is true?

    A. The slope of the line represents the down payment
    B. The slope of the line represents the monthly payment
    C. The y-intercept of the line represents the monthly payment
    D. None of the above

(Average) (Skill 6.2)

22. The equation of the line that passes through the points (-3, -5) and (2, 10) is:

    A. $3x - y + 4 = 0$
    B. $3x + y - 4 = 0$
    C. $3x + y + 4 = 0$
    D. $3x - y - 4 = 0$

(Average) (Skill 6.4)

23. The quadratic function show below has:

    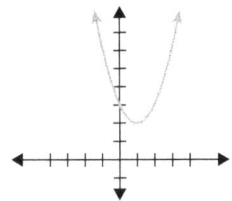

    A. Two real zeros that are equal
    B. Two real zeros that are not equal
    C. One real and one complex zero
    D. Two complex zeros

(Rigorous) (Skill 6.5)

24. The lowest point of the graph of the function $3(x - 2)^2 - 5$ is:

    A. (2, -5)
    B. (2, 5)
    C. (0, 7)
    D. (3, 5)

(Average) (Skill 6.6)

25. The vertex form of the quadratic function $x^2 + 4x + 5$ is:

    A. $(x + 1)^2 + 4$
    B. $(x - 4)^2 - 9$
    C. $(x + 2)^2 + 1$
    D. $(x - 2)^2 + 1$

(Average) (Skill 6.7)

26. Molly's dad is 27 years older than her. The product of their ages is 350 more than twice Molly's age. This can be modeled using the following equation:

    A. $x + 27 = 2x + 350$
    B. $x^2 + 25x - 350 = 0$
    C. $x^2 + 29x + 350 = 0$
    D. $x(x + 27) = 350$

(Average) (Skill 7.1)

27. The algebraic representation of the function that is the sum of 5 and the square root of the sum of x and 3 is:

    A. $5 + \sqrt{x} + 3$
    B. $(5 + x) + \sqrt{3}$
    C. $\sqrt{5 + x} + 3$
    D. $5 + \sqrt{x + 3}$

(Average) (Skill 7.2)

28. The domain and range of the polynomial function shown in the graph are:

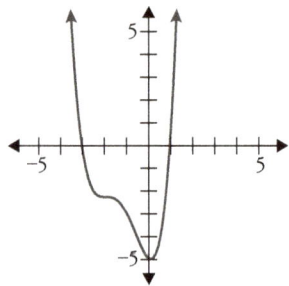

A. Domain: all x, Range: $y \geq -5$

B. Domain: $x \geq -3$, Range: $y \geq -5$

C. Domain: $y \geq -5$, Range: $x \geq -3$

D. None of the above

(Rigorous) (Skill 7.3)

29. The graph shown below represents the function:

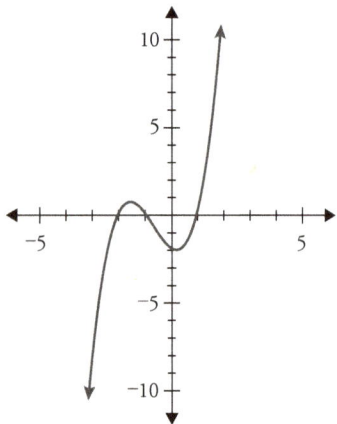

A. $2x^2 - x + 4$

B. $x^3 + 2x^2 - x - 2$

C. $x^4 + 2x^2 + 3x - 2$

D. $\sqrt{x - 2} + 5$

(Rigorous) (Skill 7.4)

30. The function $y = \frac{x + 2}{x^2 + 3x - 10}$ has one or more asymptotes at:

A. $x = -2$

B. $x = 3.3$

C. $x = 2$ and $x = -5$

D. $x = -3$ and $x = 10$

(Rigorous) (Skill 7.6)

31. Solve $\frac{2}{x + 1} = \frac{x}{1 - x^2}$.

A. $x = -1$

B. $x = -1, \frac{2}{3}$

C. $x = \frac{2}{3}$

D. There are no solutions

(Rigorous) (Skill 7.7)

32. Sam and Max are brothers. The difference in their heights is not more than 1.5 feet. If Max's height is 4.5 feet, what is Sam's height x in feet?

A. $x = 6$

B. $x = 3$

C. $3 < x < 6$

D. $x > 6$

(Rigorous) (Skill 8.1)

33. The graph shown below represents the following function:

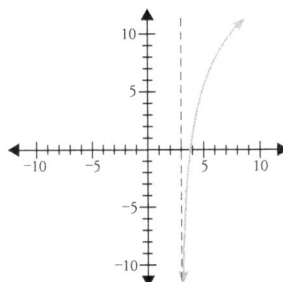

A. $\ln x + 3$

B. $\ln x - 3$

C. $5 \ln(x - 3) + 3$

D. $\ln(x + 3) + 5$

(Rigorous) (Skill 8.2)

34. The function $y = ab^{-x} + c$, where a, b, and c are constants, has:

A. A y-intercept at $y = a + c$ and a horizontal asymptote at $y = c$

B. A y-intercept at $y = c$ and no horizontal asymptote

C. A y-intercept at $y = a + c$ and no horizontal asymptote

D. A y-intercept at $y = a + c$ and a horizontal asymptote at $y = a$

(Rigorous) (Skill 8.3)

35. If $\log_a x = c$ and $\log_b x = d$, then $\log_b a$ is equal to:

A. $\frac{c}{d}$

B. $\frac{d}{c}$

C. cd

D. None of the above

(Rigorous) (Skill 8.4)

36. Solve $e^{2x} - 3e^x + 2 = 0$.

A. $x = 1, 2$

B. $x = \ln 2$

C. $x = 0$

D. $x = \ln 2, 0$

(Rigorous) (Skill 8.8)

37. A lump of dough has been placed in a warm oven to rise. For several hours the volume of the dough increases by 50% every half hour. If the initial volume of the dough is V_0, the volume V after t hours is given by:

A. $V = V_0(1.5)^{2t}$

B. $V = V_0(0.5)^{2t}$

C. $V = V_0(1.5)^t$

D. $V = V_0(0.5)^t$

(Easy) (Skill 9.1)

38. The sine function corresponding to a point on the unit circle has a positive value in quadrants:

A. I and II

B. I and III

C. I and IV

D. II and IV

POSTTEST

(Rigorous) (Skill 9.3)

39. The graph shown below represents the function:

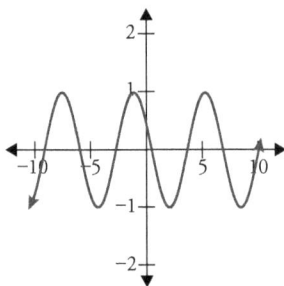

A. $\cos(x)$

B. $\cos\left(\frac{\pi}{3}x\right)$

C. $\cos\left(\frac{\pi}{3} + x\right)$

D. $\cos\left(\frac{\pi}{3} - x\right)$

(Average) (Skill 9.4)

40. A ramp is used to load boxes onto a truck. If the bed of the truck is 4 feet above the ground and the ramp is 6 feet long, what angle does the ramp make with the ground?

A. 42°

B. 48°

C. 34°

D. 60°

(Rigorous) (Skill 9.5)

41. Solve $\tan x + \cot x = 4$.

A. 60°

B. 45°

C. 30°

D. 15°

(Rigorous) (Skill 9.6)

42. The motion of a pendulum is modeled by the function $5\sin\left(\frac{\pi t}{3}\right)$ where t is the time in seconds. What is the period of the pendulum's swing?

A. 3 seconds

B. 5 seconds

C. 6 seconds

D. 15 seconds

(Average) (Skill 10.1)

43. A function $f(x)$ is continuous at $x = a$ if:

I. $f(a)$ is defined

II. $\lim_{x \to a} f(x)$ exists

III. $\lim_{x \to a} f(x) = f(a)$

A. I only

B. I and II

C. I, II, and III

D. None of the above

(Average) (Skill 10.1)

44. In the graph shown below, the average rate of change of the function between points A and B is given by:

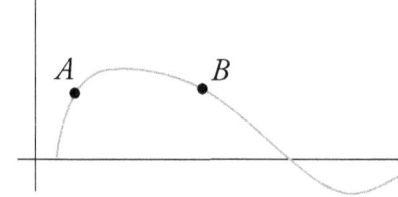

A. The slope of the tangent at point A

B. The slope of the tangent at point B

C. The slope of the line joining A and B

D. None of the above

(Average) (Skill 10.3)

45. In the graph of the function $f(x)$ shown below, at point A:

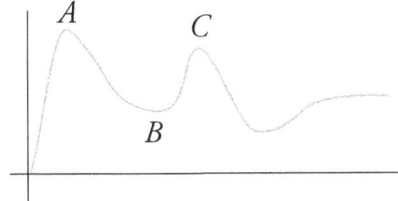

A. $f'(x) = 0$ and $f''(x) = 0$

B. $f'(x) = 0$ and $f''(x) > 0$

C. $f'(x) = 0$ and $f''(x) < 0$

D. $f'(x) < 0$ and $f''(x) < 0$

(Rigorous) (Skill 10.4)

46. The function $\frac{x^3}{3} + \frac{x^2}{2} + x$ is the indefinite integral of the function:

A. $x^2 + x + 1$

B. $\frac{x^4}{12} + \frac{x^3}{6} + \frac{x^2}{2}$

C. $\frac{x^2}{2} + x$

D. $\frac{x^3}{3} + \frac{x^2}{2}$

(Rigorous) (Skill 10.5)

47. The work done by a force $F(x)$ applied on an object from position $x = 0$ to $x = a$ is given by the integral $\int_0^a F(x)dx$. If $F(x) = mx + n$, where m and n are constants, what is the work done when the force $F(x)$ is applied from $x = 0$ to $x = a$?

A. $ma + n$

B. $\frac{1}{2}ma^2$

C. $\frac{1}{2}ma^2 + na$

D. $\frac{1}{2}ma^2 + n$

(Average) (Skill 11.1)

48. Acceleration is the rate of change of speed, which has the units m/s (meters/second). What is the unit for the rate of change of acceleration?

A. m/s^2

B. m/s^3

C. m^2/s

D. m^2/s^2

(Average) (Skill 11.2)

49. A cylinder and a cone both have the same radius and the same height. What is the ratio of the volume of the cylinder to the volume of the cone?

A. 3

B. $\frac{1}{3}$

C. $\frac{1}{2}$

D. 4

(Easy) (Skill 11.3)

50. The side of a cube is increased by a factor of 1.5. Its volume is increased by a factor of:

A. 1.5

B. 2.25

C. 3.375

D. 4.525

(Easy) (Skill 11.4)

51. A 30°-60°-90° triangle has a hypotenuse 15 cm long. What is the length of its shortest side?

   A. 7.5 cm
   B. 5 cm
   C. 8.66 cm
   D. 1.73 cm

(Rigorous) (Skill 11.6)

52. Find the area enclosed by the parabola $f(x) = x^2$ and the line $y = 4$.

   A. $\frac{8}{3}$
   B. $\frac{10}{3}$
   C. $\frac{20}{3}$
   D. 5

(Easy) (Skill 12.2)

53. What is the minimum number of noncollinear points needed to define a plane?

   A. 1
   B. 2
   C. 3
   D. 4

(Easy) (Skill 12.3)

54. Triangles bounded by parallel lines, as shown below, have the same:

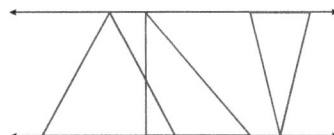

   A. Base
   B. Height
   C. Area
   D. Angles

(Average) (Skill 12.4)

55. In the diagram shown below, $AB \cong BC$ and DB bisects $\angle ABC$. The triangles DAB and DCB can be proven to be congruent using:

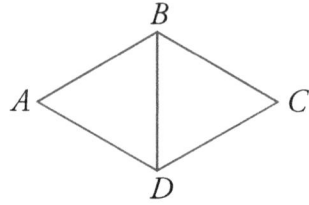

   A. SSS
   B. SAS
   C. AAS
   D. HL

(Average) (Skill 12.5)

56. The purpose of the construction shown below is to:

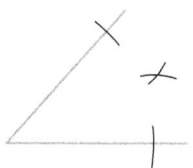

   A. Draw a perpendicular line to one of the sides
   B. Bisect the angle
   C. Trisect the angle
   D. Draw a right triangle

(Average) (Skill 12.7)

57. Euclid's fifth axiom, the parallel postulate:

   I. Can be proven using the other axioms
   II. Does not hold for non-Euclidean geometries

   A. Only I is true
   B. Only II is true
   C. Both I and II are true
   D. Neither I nor II is true

(Average) (Skill 13.1)

58. A regular polygon with each interior angle equal to 108 degrees is a(n):

   A. Pentagon
   B. Hexagon
   C. Heptagon
   D. Octagon

(Average) (Skill 13.2)

59. When two chords intersect inside a circle and each chord is divided into two smaller segments:

   A. The sum of the lengths of the two segments formed from one chord equals the sum of the lengths of the two segments formed from the other chord
   B. The chords bisect each other
   C. The chords are perpendicular to each other
   D. The product of the lengths of the two segments formed from one chord equals the product of the lengths of the two segments formed from the other chord

(Rigorous) (Skill 13.3)

60. Which of the following three-dimensional figures does not belong with the others?

   cone, cylinder, rectangular prism, triangular prism

   A. Cone
   B. Cylinder
   C. Rectangular prism
   D. Triangular prism

(Average) (Skill 13.4)

61. The perimeter of the composite figure shown is:

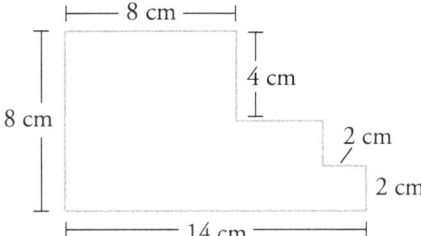

   A. 28 cm
   B. 32 cm
   C. 38 cm
   D. 44 cm

(Rigorous) (Skill 13.5)

62. Which of the following cross-sections can be obtained by cutting through a right circular cylinder?

   I. Circle
   II. Ellipse
   III. Rectangle

   A. I only
   B. I and II
   C. I and III
   D. I, II, and III

(Easy) (Skill 13.7)

63. A 20-foot by 18-foot room is to be covered with hardwood flooring. The flooring material comes in planks of different sizes. Which of the following available sizes may be used to cover the area with minimum wastage?

   A. 3 ft. by 5 ft.
   B. 3 ft. by 7 ft.
   C. 4 ft. by 4 ft.
   D. 4 ft. by 8 ft.

(Average) (Skill 14.1)

64. Which of the following geometric transformations retains both the original size and original orientation of an object?

   A. Reflection
   B. Rotation
   C. Translation
   D. Dilation

(Average) (Skill 14.3)

65. A rectangle is symmetric under which of the following rotations in the plane?

   I. 90°
   II. 180°
   III. 360°

   A. I
   B. I and II
   C. II and III
   D. I, II, and III

(Rigorous) (Skill 14.4)

66. A square with corners at (−3, 3), (3, 3), (3, −3), and (−3, −3) on the coordinate plane is dilated with a scale factor of 2 and the center of dilation at the origin. The corners of the transformed square are at:

   A. (−6, 6), (6, 6), (3, −3), and (−3, −3)
   B. (−3, 3), (3, 3), (6, −6), and (−6, −6)
   C. (−3, 3), (3, 3), (9, −9), and (−9, −9)
   D. (−6, 6), (6, 6), (6, −6), and (−6, −6)

(Rigorous) (Skill 14.5)

67. A quadrilateral has corners at (−3, 3), (3, 3), (0, −3), and (6, −3) on the coordinate plane. Which of the following is true?

   I. The quadrilateral is a parallelogram
   II. The diagonals of the quadrilateral are perpendicular to each other

   A. I only
   B. II only
   C. I and II
   D. Neither I nor II

(Rigorous) (Skill 14.6)

68. The equation $ax^2 + by^2 = c^2$, where a, b, and c are constants, is the equation of a circle if:

   A. $a = b, c > 0$
   B. $a = b, a > 0, b > 0$
   C. $a = b = c$
   D. $a = b, a < 0, b < 0$

(Rigorous) (Skill 14.8)

69. Vectors $ai + bj$ and $ci + dj$ (where a, b, c, d are constants) are perpendicular to each other when:

    A. $ab = cd$

    B. $ac = bd$

    C. $ac + bd = 0$

    D. $ad + bc = 0$

(Average) (Skill 15.1)

70. A survey is conducted to collect data about preferred ice cream flavors. People are asked to rank five flavors in order of preference. The kind of measurement scale used is:

    A. Nominal

    B. Ordinal

    C. Interval

    D. Ratio

(Easy) (Skill 15.1)

71. In a box-and-whisker plot, the box is drawn from:

    A. The first quartile to the median

    B. The median to the third quartile

    C. The first quartile to the third quartile

    D. None of the above

(Average) (Skill 15.3)

72. The data distribution shown below is:

    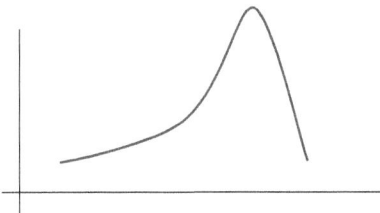

    A. Symmetric

    B. Skewed to the left

    C. Skewed to the right

    D. Bimodal

(Rigorous) (Skill 15.4)

73. In the data distribution shown in question 72:

    A. The mean and mode are both at the peak

    B. The mean is to the left of the mode

    C. The mean is to the right of the mode

    D. Both the mean and median are to the left of the peak

(Rigorous) (Skill 15.5)

74. The following linear transformation indicates a simple translation of the data without any stretching or shrinking:

    A. $X' = X + 3$

    B. $X' = 2X + 3$

    C. $X' = 5X + 1$

    D. $X' = 3X$

(Rigorous) (Skill 15.6)

75. The measure of central tendency most affected by including an outlier in a data set is the:

    A. Median
    B. Mean
    C. Mode
    D. Mean and mode

(Rigorous) (Skill 16.1)

76. A coin tossing experiment yields five heads in a row. This indicates that:

    A. There is a lower chance of getting a head in the next toss
    B. The coin is weighted
    C. The experimental procedure is flawed
    D. None of the above

(Easy) (Skill 16.2)

77. Melanie, Maria, Ethel, Elizabeth, Rita, Gilda, and Renee put their names in a hat and draw one name to decide who will pay for everybody's lunch. What is the probability that a name without an "e" in it will be drawn?

    A. $\frac{3}{7}$
    B. $\frac{4}{7}$
    C. $\frac{2}{7}$
    D. $\frac{5}{7}$

(Rigorous) (Skill 16.4)

78. A drawer has 3 blue socks, 8 red socks, and 5 green socks in it. If 3 socks are pulled out of the drawer at random, what is the probability that all 3 are blue?

    A. $\frac{3}{16}$
    B. $\frac{1}{560}$
    C. $\frac{1}{1120}$
    D. $\frac{1}{1680}$

(Rigorous) (Skill 16.5)

79. A dart board has a square in the center of a circle. If the side of the square is 7 inches and the probability of a dart hitting the square is 0.3, what is the radius of the circle in inches?

    A. 7.2
    B. 2.1
    C. 23.3
    D. 14.0

(Average) (Skill 16.6)

80. In a high school class of 30 children, 10 take French, 12 take Spanish, and 3 take both French and Spanish. What is the probability that a student chosen at random from the class takes French or Spanish?

    A. $\frac{11}{15}$
    B. $\frac{2}{15}$
    C. $\frac{19}{30}$
    D. $\frac{25}{30}$

(Rigorous) (Skill 16.7)

81. The expected value of a random variable is:

    A. The mean value that would be obtained from an infinite number of observations

    B. The average of possible values weighted by the probability of each

    C. The integral of a continuous random variable multiplied by its probability density function over its range of values

    D. All of the above

(Easy) (Skill 17.1)

82. To study how effective a drug is in treating a disease, the best method of data collection is a(n):

    A. Census

    B. Sample survey

    C. Controlled experiment

    D. Observational study

(Average) (Skill 17.2)

83. Most of the employees in a company earn less than $100,000. The CEO earns $1,000,000. An article about the company states that the average salary is $110,000. Which of the following statements are correct?

    I. The information in the article is not misleading since $110,000 is the actual average amount earned by company employees.

    II. The information in the article is misleading since an outlier has been included in calculating the average.

    III. Instead of the mean, a different measure of central tendency such as the median should have been selected.

    A. I and II

    B. I and III

    C. II and III

    D. I, II, and III

(Average) (Skill 17.3)

84. In a survey, the sample is chosen such that all racial groups are represented.

    What is this method of sampling called?

    A. Random

    B. Systematic

    C. Stratified

    D. Cluster

POSTTEST

(Rigorous) (Skill 17.4)

85. What is the probability of getting 7 heads in a series of 10 coin flips?

   A. 0.12
   B. 0.5
   C. 0.7
   D. 0.9

(Average) (Skill 17.5)

86. Given the following set of (x, y) points, which regression line best fits the data?

   (0, 0), (1, 0.6), (2, 1.25), (3, 2.1), (4, 2.5)

   A. $y = \frac{1}{20}x$
   B. $y = -\frac{1}{20}x$
   C. $y = \frac{2}{3}x$
   D. $y = -\frac{2}{3}x$

(Rigorous) (Skill 17.6)

87. In order to fit to the exponential regression function $y = ae^{bx}$, nonlinear data can be transformed to linear form by:

   A. Taking the reciprocal
   B. Taking the natural logarithm
   C. Taking the square root
   D. Squaring

(Average) (Skill 18.1)

88. In a mathematical proof, a premise is:

   A. A given statement that is true
   B. A given statement that is assumed to be true
   C. A given statement that is false but is assumed to be true
   D. Reasoning provided to support a statement

(Average) (Skill 18.2)

89. The conclusion "Alex is a swimmer" can be drawn from the following premises:

   A. All boys from East high school are swimmers. Alex is a student at East high school.
   B. One of the students at East high school is a swimmer. Alex is one of the students at East high school.
   C. All students from East high school are swimmers. Alex is a student at East high school.
   D. All of the above

(Rigorous) (Skill 18.3)

90. Matilda has left her home with an umbrella every morning for a week. One can use inductive reasoning to conjecture that:

   I. Matilda will leave home with an umbrella the next morning
   II. It has been raining every morning for a week

   A. I only
   B. II only
   C. I and II
   D. Neither I nor II

(Easy) (Skill 18.5)

91. Guess-and-check is:

   A. A valid strategy for solving a math problem
   B. A strategy used to understand a problem which must be solved using a different method
   C. An invalid method of problem-solving since it does not show understanding of concepts
   D. An invalid method of problem-solving since it does not follow logical steps

(Average) (Skill 19.1)

92. The points (0, 3) and (5, 3) can be used to represent:

    A. A horizontal line
    B. The side of a square
    C. The side of a triangle
    D. All of the above

(Easy) (Skill 19.3)

93. The equation $y = \frac{3}{x}$ can be expressed verbally as:

    I. y is equal to 3 divided by x
    II. y is equal to 3 times the reciprocal of x
    III. The product of x and y is equal to 3

    A. I only
    B. I and II
    C. I and III
    D. I, II, and III

(Easy) (Skill 19.4)

94. This type of mathematical representation is typically not used in high school mathematics:

    A. Symbolic
    B. Pictorial
    C. Concrete
    D. Graphical

(Easy) (Skill 19.5)

95. A science project requires students to compare how rainfall patterns change from January to December for two consecutive years. The best way to analyze this information is to represent it:

    A. In table form
    B. As line graphs on the same coordinate axes with the lines drawn using different colors
    C. With separate pie charts for each year showing one month in each segment
    D. With bars of different colors on the same chart showing the rainfall for each month

(Average) (Skill 20.4)

96. Stopwatches can be used in the mathematics classroom to enhance students' understanding of the concept of:

    A. Measurement
    B. Intervals
    C. Precision
    D. Accuracy

(Average) (Skill 20.5)

97. A teacher is introducing the concept of linear relationships to her class using equations, real-life examples, and tables and graphs. In what order should each of these instructional elements be introduced?

    A. Equations, real-life examples, tables and graphs
    B. Real-life examples, tables and graphs, equations
    C. Real-life examples, equations, tables and graphs
    D. Equations, tables and graphs, real-life examples

POSTTEST

(Average) (Skill 20.8)

98. **Which of the following kinds of questioning strategies requires the highest level of thinking?**

    A. Synthesis of disparate information

    B. Test of knowledge

    C. Analysis of a concept into component parts

    D. Test of comprehension

(Easy) (Skill 21.1)

99. **The purpose of a summative assessment is:**

    A. To assess whether a student is able to think outside the box

    B. To gather information so instruction can be improved

    C. To assess whether a student has met learning goals at the end of a unit

    D. To get an informal sense of how much a student knows

(Average) (Skill 21.4)

100. **In order to use the results of assessments to improve instruction, a teacher must:**

    A. Assess prior knowledge of students

    B. Use frequent assessment strategies of different kinds

    C. Have a flexible instructional plan that can be modified

    D. All of the above

Posttest Answer Key

1. D	11. B	21. B	31. C	41. D	51. A	61. D	71. C	81. D	91. A
2. C	12. A	22. A	32. C	42. C	52. C	62. D	72. B	82. C	92. D
3. D	13. C	23. D	33. C	43. C	53. C	63. A	73. B	83. C	93. D
4. B	14. C	24. A	34. A	44. C	54. B	64. C	74. A	84. C	94. C
5. B	15. D	25. C	35. B	45. C	55. B	65. C	75. B	85. A	95. B
6. A	16. A	26. B	36. D	46. A	56. B	66. D	76. D	86. C	96. C
7. B	17. A	27. D	37. A	47. C	57. B	67. A	77. A	87. B	97. B
8. C	18. A	28. A	38. A	48. B	58. A	68. B	78. B	88. B	98. A
9. A	19. B	29. B	39. C	49. A	59. D	69. C	79. A	89. C	99. C
10. C	20. D	30. C	40. A	50. C	60. A	70. B	80. C	90. A	100. D

Posttest Rigor Table

Rigor level	Questions
Easy 20%	1, 8, 9, 10, 11, 12, 38, 50, 51, 53, 54, 63, 71, 77, 82, 91, 93, 94, 95, 99
Average 39%	2, 3, 4, 14, 15, 16, 22, 23, 25, 26, 27, 28, 40, 43, 44, 45, 48, 49, 55, 56, 57, 58, 59, 61, 64, 65, 70, 72, 80, 83, 84, 86, 88, 89, 92, 96, 97, 98, 100
Rigorous 41%	5, 6, 7, 13, 17, 18, 19, 20, 21, 24, 29, 30, 31, 32, 33, 34, 35, 36, 37, 39, 41, 42, 46, 47, 52, 60, 62, 66, 67, 68, 69, 73, 74, 75, 76, 78, 79, 81, 85, 87, 90

Posttest Answers with Rationales

(Easy) (Skill 1.1)
1. The digit 3 in the number 129.0035 is in the:

   A. Hundreds place
   B. Hundredths place
   C. Thousands place
   D. Thousandths place

   Answer: D. Thousandths place

   The value of the digit 3 in the number 129.0035 is $\frac{3}{1000}$, i.e., three thousandths. It is in the thousandths place.

(Average) (Skill 1.3)
2. Which property of real numbers is used in going from Step 1 to Step 2?

   Step 1: $(3a + 4) + -4 = 12$

   Step 2: $3a + (4 + -4) = 12$

   A. Inverse property
   B. Identity property
   C. Associative property
   D. Commutative property

   Answer: C. Associative property

   According to the associative property of addition, for all real numbers a, b, and c, $(a + b) + c = a + (b + c)$; i.e., the result of two consecutive additions is independent of the order in which the operations are carried out.

(Average) (Skill 1.4)
3. The distance from the earth to the sun is 90 million miles. Which of the following expresses this number correctly in scientific notation?

   A. 90,000,000
   B. 90×10^6
   C. 9.0×10^6
   D. 9.0×10^7

   Answer: D. 9.0×10^7

   In scientific notation there must be only one digit to the left of the decimal point. Option C meets this requirement but represents the number 9 million, not 90 million.

(Average) (Skill 1.6)
4. Reena ate one-third of all the candy pieces she received when trick-or-treating on Halloween. She gave half the remaining candy to her brother. If six pieces of candy are left over, how many pieces of candy did Reena have in the beginning?

   A. 36
   B. 18
   C. 12
   D. 24

   Answer: B. 18

   This problem must be solved by working backward. Just before Reena gave candy to her brother she had $6 \times 2 = 12$ pieces of candy. This is two-thirds of the total number of pieces she had in the beginning. Since she ate one-third of the candy, she ate $12 \div 2 = 6$ pieces.

Therefore, the number of pieces of candy she had in the beginning $= 12 + 6 = 18$.

(Rigorous) (Skill 2.2)

5. **Which of the following complex numbers have the same modulus?**

   $3 + 4i, -5 + 2i, 4 + \sqrt{13}i, \sqrt{5} - 6i$

   A. $3 + 4i$ and $-5 + 2i$
   B. $-5 + 2i$ and $4 + \sqrt{13}i$
   C. $4 + \sqrt{13}i$ and $\sqrt{5} - 6i$
   D. $3 + 4i$ and $\sqrt{5} - 6i$

   Answer: B. $-5 + 2i$ and $4 + \sqrt{13}i$

   The modulus of $-5 + 2i = \sqrt{(-5)^2 + 2^2} = \sqrt{25 + 4} = \sqrt{29}$.

   The modulus of $4 + \sqrt{13}i = \sqrt{(4)^2 + (\sqrt{13})^2} = \sqrt{16 + 13} = \sqrt{29}$.

(Rigorous) (Skill 2.4)

6. **Which of the following complex operations is represented in the vector diagram below?**

   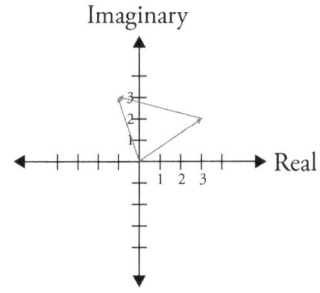

   A. $(3 + 2i) + (-4 + i) = -1 + 3i$
   B. $(3 + 2i) + (-1 + 3i) = 2 + 5i$
   C. $(3 + 2i) \times (-4 + i) = -1 + 3i$
   D. $(3 + 2i) + (-4 + i) = 3 - i$

   Answer: A. $(3 + 2i) + (-4 + i) = -1 + 3i$

   Options C and D show operations that are incorrect, so the answer choices cannot be the right ones. The diagram shows vector addition with the two vectors on the right added to get the vector on the left as a resultant. Inspection of the diagram shows that the vectors added are $3 + 2i$ and $-4 + i$ with the resultant being $-1 + 3i$.

(Rigorous) (Skill 2.5)

7. **The complex numbers $1 + 2i$ and $1 - 2i$ are roots of the quadratic equation:**

   A. $x^2 + 4 = 0$
   B. $x^2 - 2x + 5 = 0$
   C. $x^2 + 2x + 5 = 0$
   D. $x^2 - 2 = 0$

   Answer: B. $x^2 - 2x + 5 = 0$

   $(x - (1 + 2i))$ and $(x - (1 - 2i))$ are factors of the quadratic function that has $1 + 2i$ and $1 - 2i$ as zeros. Since a quadratic function has exactly two zeros, it can be written as the product of the two factors $(x - (1 + 2i))(x - (1 - 2i))$
   $= (x - 1 - 2i)(x - 1 + 2i)$
   $= (x - 1)^2 - (2i)^2$
   $= x^2 - 2x + 1 + 4$
   $= x^2 - 2x + 5$.

(Easy) (Skill 3.1)

8. **Find the GCF of 12, 42, and 78.**

   A. 2
   B. 4
   C. 6
   D. 12

   Answer: C. 6

   The prime factorizations of the given numbers are $12 = 2^2 \cdot 3$, $42 = 2 \cdot 3 \cdot 7$, $78 = 2 \cdot 3 \cdot 13$.

   The only factors all three have in common are 2 and 3. Therefore the GCF = $2 \cdot 3 = 6$.

(Easy) (Skill 3.3)

9. **Find the sum of the following matrices:**

   $\begin{pmatrix} 6 & 3 \\ 9 & 15 \end{pmatrix} \begin{pmatrix} 4 & 7 \\ 1 & 0 \end{pmatrix}$

   A. $\begin{pmatrix} 10 & 10 \\ 10 & 15 \end{pmatrix}$
   B. $\begin{pmatrix} 13 & 7 \\ 9 & 16 \end{pmatrix}$
   C. 45
   D. $\begin{pmatrix} 20 \\ 25 \end{pmatrix}$

   Answer: A. $\begin{pmatrix} 10 & 10 \\ 10 & 15 \end{pmatrix}$

   Two matrices with the same dimensions are added by adding the corresponding elements. In this case, element 1,1 (i.e., row 1, column 1) of the first matrix is added to element 1,1 of the second matrix; element 2,1 of the first matrix is added to element 2,1 of the second matrix; and so on for all four elements.

(Easy) (Skill 3.3)

10. **The product of two matrices can be found only if:**

    A. The number of rows in the first matrix is equal to the number of rows in the second matrix
    B. The number of columns in the first matrix is equal to the number of columns in the second matrix
    C. The number of columns in the first matrix is equal to the number of rows in the second matrix
    D. The number of rows in the first matrix is equal to the number of columns in the second matrix

    Answer: C. The number of columns in the first matrix is equal to the number of rows in the second matrix

    The number of columns in the first matrix must equal the number of rows in the second matrix because the process of multiplication involves multiplying the elements of every row of the first matrix with corresponding elements of every column of the second matrix.

ANSWERS WITH RATIONALES

(Easy) (Skill 3.3)

11. Which of the following properties does *not* apply to matrix multiplication?

    A. Associativity
    B. Commutativity
    C. Distributivity
    D. All of the above

Answer: B. Commutativity

Matrix multiplication obeys associativity and distributivity but not commutativity, as shown below.

$$\begin{pmatrix} a & b \\ c & d \end{pmatrix} \begin{pmatrix} e & f \\ g & h \end{pmatrix} = \begin{pmatrix} ae - bg & af - bh \\ ce - dg & cf - dh \end{pmatrix}$$

$$\begin{pmatrix} e & f \\ g & h \end{pmatrix} \begin{pmatrix} a & b \\ c & d \end{pmatrix} = \begin{pmatrix} ae - cf & be - df \\ ag - ch & bg - dh \end{pmatrix}$$

Obviously, the two products are different.

(Easy) (Skill 3.4)

12. Ron bakes a cake using a recipe that calls for 5 cups of flour and 4 cups of sugar. When he measures out the flour he finds that he only has $4\frac{1}{2}$ cups. How many cups of sugar should he use?

    A. $3\frac{3}{5}$
    B. $3\frac{1}{2}$
    C. 5
    D. $3\frac{4}{5}$

Answer: A. $3\frac{3}{5}$

Let x be the number of cups of sugar to be used with 4.5 cups of flour. Set up a proportion equation: $\frac{5}{4.5} = \frac{4}{x}$.

Cross-multiplying: $5x = 4(4.5) \Rightarrow 5x = 18 \Rightarrow x = \frac{18}{5} = 3\frac{3}{5}$.

(Rigorous) (Skill 4.1)

13. Which of the following graphs is the next in the sequence of graphs shown below?

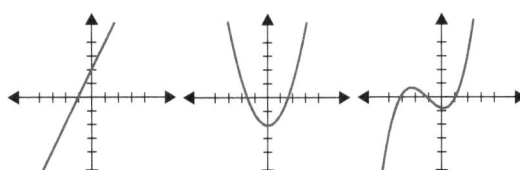

A.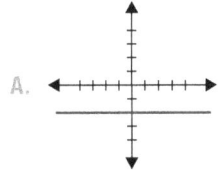

B.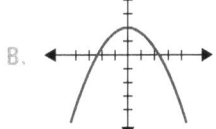

C.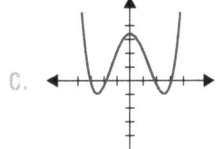

D.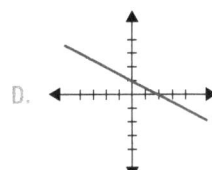

Answer: C.

The graphs shown in the sequence are of polynomials in increasing powers of x: linear, quadratic, and third order. This becomes clear if one notes the number of times each graph crosses the x-axis, which indicates the number of zeros of the function. The next graph, therefore, must be a fourth-order function of x with four zeros. Option C matches this criterion.

(Average) (Skill 4.3)

14. To prove by mathematical induction that $1^2 + 3^2 + 5^2 + ... + (2N − 1)^2 = N^2$, one must first show that this is true for $N = 1$ and also that:

    A. It is true for $N = 2, 3, 4, 5,$ and 6
    B. It is true for $N = k$ and for $N = k + 1$
    C. If it is true for $N = k$, then it is also true for $N = k + 1$
    D. None of the above

Answer: C. If it is true for $N = k$, then it is also true for $N = k + 1$

Proof by induction states that a statement is true for all numbers if the following two statements can be proven:

1. The statement is true for $n = 1$.

2. If the statement is true for $n = k$, then it is also true for $n = k + 1$.

(Average) (Skill 4.4)

15. The sequence given below is:

    $\{\frac{2}{3}, \frac{2}{5}, \frac{6}{25}, \frac{18}{125}, ...\}$

    A. An arithmetic series with common difference $\frac{4}{15}$
    B. An arithmetic series with common ratio $\frac{3}{5}$
    C. A geometric series with common difference $\frac{4}{15}$
    D. A geometric series with common ratio $\frac{3}{5}$

Answer: D. A geometric series with common ratio $\frac{3}{5}$

Inspection of the sequence shows that each term is obtained by multiplying the previous one by $\frac{3}{5}$. This is, therefore, a geometric series with common ratio $\frac{3}{5}$.

(Average) (Skill 5.1)

16. The list of (x, y) points given below represents:

    $\{(1, 5), (3, 2), (-1, 4), (1, 2), (2, 5)\}$

    A. A relation with domain $\{-1, 1, 2, 3\}$
    B. A function with domain $\{-1, 1, 2, 3\}$
    C. A relation with domain $\{2, 4, 5\}$
    D. A function with domain $\{2, 4, 5\}$

Answer: A. A relation with domain $\{-1, 1, 2, 3\}$

A relation is a set of ordered pairs like the one shown above. The first number of each pair forms the domain while the second number of each pair forms the range. In this case the domain is $\{-1, 1, 2, 3\}$ and the range is $\{2, 4, 5\}$. A function is a relation in which each element of the domain is paired with one and only one element of the range. In this case $x = 1$ is paired with both $y = 5$ and $y = 2$. Therefore, the relation represented here is not a function.

(Rigorous) (Skill 5.2)

17. What is the domain of the function $\frac{x+1}{x^2+2x-3}$?

   A. $x \neq -3, 1$

   B. $x \neq 3, -1$

   C. $x \neq -\frac{3}{2}$

   D. All values of x

Answer: A. $x \neq -3, 1$

The domain of a rational function x excludes x values that reduce the denominator to zero. In this case, the domain includes all x values except for those that are solutions to the equation $x^2 + 2x - 3 = 0$. This can be solved by factoring: $x^2 + 2x - 3 = (x+3)(x-1) = 0 \Rightarrow x = -3$ *or* 1. Therefore the domain of the function excludes the values $x = -3$ and $x = 1$.

(Rigorous) (Skill 5.5)

18. If a transformation of the form $f(x - k) + m$, where k and m are positive numbers, is applied to a function $f(x)$, the graph of the function will be displaced:

   A. Upward and toward the right

   B. Upward and toward the left

   C. Downward and toward the right

   D. Downward and toward the left

Answer: A. Upward and toward the right

Adding m units to the function clearly displaces it upward. Replacing x with $x - k$ in effect makes the point in the graph that corresponds to $x = 0$ correspond to $x - k = 0 \Rightarrow x = k$, which is a shift to the right.

(Rigorous) (Skill 5.6)

19. Which of the following functions does *not* have an inverse?

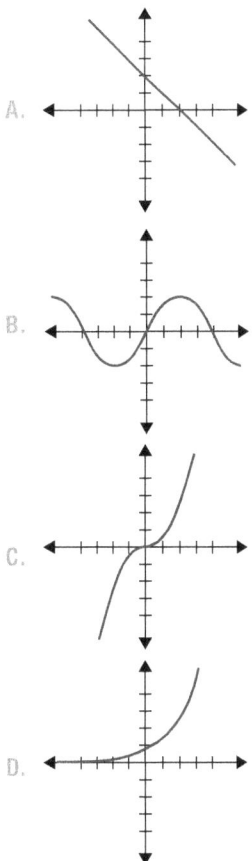

Answer: B.

A function has an inverse only if it is a one-to-one function, i.e., each value of x corresponds to only one value of y and vice versa. In other words, the function must pass both the vertical and horizontal line tests, i.e., any vertical or horizontal line drawn on the graph must intersect it at only one point. Option B clearly fails the horizontal line test.

POSTTEST

(Rigorous) (Skill 5.7)

20. Which of the following functions share the same graphical representation?

    I. $\ln x + \ln x^3$

    II. $4 \ln x$

    III. $\ln(e^{4 \ln x})$

    A. I and II
    B. I and III
    C. II and III
    D. I, II, and III

    Answer: D. I, II, and III

    All three functions share the same graphical representation because they are identical to each other:
    $\ln x + \ln x^3 = \ln x + 3 \ln x = 4 \ln x$
    $\ln(e^{4 \ln x}) = 4 \ln x \ln(e) = 4 \ln x$.

(Rigorous) (Skill 6.1)

21. Debbie finances a house with a $10,000 down payment and a monthly payment of $700. The total payment y made after x months is expressed as a linear function $y = f(x)$ that is plotted on a coordinate plane. Which of the following is true?

    A. The slope of the line represents the down payment
    B. The slope of the line represents the monthly payment
    C. The y-intercept of the line represents the monthly payment
    D. None of the above

    Answer: B. The slope of the line represents the monthly payment

    The function representing the total payment can be written as $y = 700x + 10,000$. This is in the form $y = mx + b$ where m is the slope and b is the y-intercept. Hence, the slope represents the monthly payment and the y-intercept represents the down payment.

(Average) (Skill 6.2)

22. The equation of the line that passes through the points (-3, -5) and (2, 10) is:

    A. $3x - y + 4 = 0$
    B. $3x + y - 4 = 0$
    C. $3x + y + 4 = 0$
    D. $3x - y - 4 = 0$

    Answer: A. $3x - y + 4 = 0$

    The slope of the line $= \frac{-5 - 10}{-3 - 2} = \frac{-15}{-5} = 3$. Therefore, the equation in the slope-intercept form is $y = 3x + b$ where b is the y-intercept. The value of b can be determined by putting the (x, y) values of one of the points into the equation: $-5 = 3(-3) + b \Rightarrow -5 = -9 + b \Rightarrow b = 4$. So the equation of the line is $y = 3x + 4$. Rearranging the terms to put the equation in standard form: $3x - y + 4 = 0$.

(Average) (Skill 6.4)

23. The quadratic function show below has:

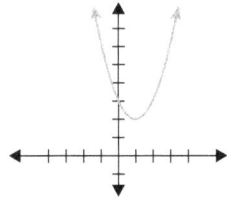

   A. Two real zeros that are equal
   B. Two real zeros that are not equal
   C. One real and one complex zero
   D. Two complex zeros

Answer: D. Two complex zeros

The real zeros of a quadratic function are the x-values of the points where the graph intersects the x-axis. Since the graph shown here does not intersect the x-axis, the function has no real zeros. Therefore the zeros of the function are both complex.

(Rigorous) (Skill 6.5)

24. The lowest point of the graph of the function $y = 3(x - 2)^2 - 5$ is:

   A. (2, -5)
   B. (2, 5)
   C. (0, 7)
   D. (3, 5)

Answer: A. (2, -5)

The vertex form of the equation of a parabola is $y = a(x - h)^2 + k$ where (h, k) is the vertex or the lowest point of a parabola that opens upward. The function $y = 3(x - 2)^2 - 5$ is expressed in vertex form where $h = 2$ and $k = -5$.

(Average) (Skill 6.6)

25. The vertex form of the quadratic function $x^2 + 4x + 5$ is:

   A. $(x + 1)^2 + 4$
   B. $(x - 4)^2 - 9$
   C. $(x + 2)^2 + 1$
   D. $(x - 2)^2 + 1$

Answer: C. $(x + 2)^2 + 1$

The function can be expressed in the vertex form by completing the square: $x^2 + 4x + 5 = x^2 + 4x + 4 + 1 = (x + 2)^2 + 1$.

(Average) (Skill 6.7)

26. Molly's dad is 27 years older than her. The product of their ages is 350 more than twice Molly's age. This can be modeled using the following equation:

   A. $x + 27 = 2x + 350$
   B. $x^2 + 25x - 350 = 0$
   C. $x^2 + 29x + 350 = 0$
   D. $x(x + 27) = 350$

Answer: B. $x^2 + 25x - 350 = 0$

Let Molly's age be x. Her dad's age is $x + 27$. The product of their ages is $x(x + 27)$. According to the problem, $x(x + 27) = 2x + 350$.

Simplifying: $x^2 + 27x = 2x + 350$ $\Rightarrow x^2 + 25x - 350 = 0$.

(Average) (Skill 7.1)

27. The algebraic representation of the function that is the sum of 5 and the square root of the sum of x and 3 is:

    A. $5 + \sqrt{x} + 3$
    B. $(5 + x) + \sqrt{3}$
    C. $\sqrt{5 + x + 3}$
    D. $5 + \sqrt{x + 3}$

    Answer: D. $5 + \sqrt{x + 3}$

    The sum of x and $3 = x + 3$.

    The square root of the sum of x and $3 = \sqrt{x + 3}$.

    The sum of 5 and the square root of the sum of x and $3 = 5 + \sqrt{x + 3}$.

(Average) (Skill 7.2)

28. The domain and range of the polynomial function shown in the graph are:

    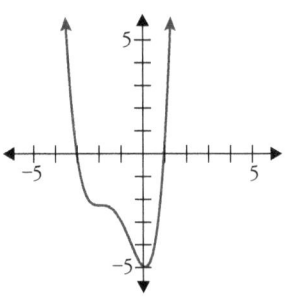

    A. Domain: all x, Range: $y \geq -5$
    B. Domain: $x \geq -3$, Range: $y \geq -5$
    C. Domain: $y \geq -5$, Range: $x \geq -3$
    D. None of the above

    Answer: A. Domain: all x, Range: $y \geq -5$

    Since this is a polynomial function, the domain includes all values of x. The graph shows that the lowest value of y is -5.

(Rigorous) (Skill 7.3)

29. The graph shown below represents the function:

    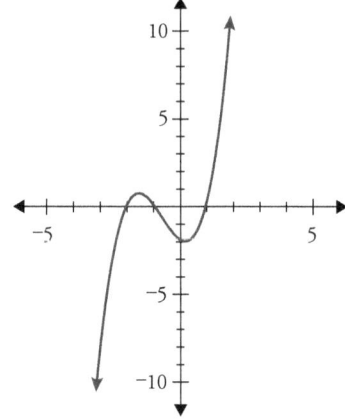

    A. $2x^2 - x + 4$
    B. $x^3 + 2x^2 - x - 2$
    C. $x^4 + 2x^2 + 3x - 2$
    D. $\sqrt{x - 2} + 5$

    Answer: B. $x^3 + 2x^2 - x - 2$

    Option D is clearly incorrect since it is a radical function with domain $x \geq 2$. Options A and C are polynomials of even order, which means that the endpoints of the graph should go in the same direction, both upward or both downward. Since one end of the graph goes upward and the other downward, the end behavior of the graph is consistent with that of a polynomial of odd order. Hence, B is the correct answer.

(Rigorous) (Skill 7.4)

30. The function $y = \frac{x+2}{x^2 + 3x - 10}$ has one or more asymptotes at:

   A. $x = -2$
   B. $x = 3.3$
   C. $x = 2$ and $x = -5$
   D. $x = -3$ and $x = 10$

   Answer: C. $x = 2$ and $x = -5$

   Vertical asymptotes are found at the zeros of the denominator of a rational function. For the given function, these zeros can be found by solving $x^2 + 3x - 10 = 0$. Factoring, we get $(x - 2)(x + 5) = 0$. Thus the vertical asymptotes of the function are at $x = 2$ and $x = -5$.

(Rigorous) (Skill 7.6)

31. Solve $\frac{2}{x+1} = \frac{x}{1-x^2}$.

   A. $x = -1$
   B. $x = -1, \frac{2}{3}$
   C. $x = \frac{2}{3}$
   D. There are no solutions

   Answer: C. $x = \frac{2}{3}$

   $\frac{2}{x+1} = \frac{x}{1-x^2}$

   Cross-multiplying and simplifying:
   $2(1 - x^2) = x(x + 1)$; $2 - 2x^2 = x^2 + x$; $3x^2 + x - 2 = 0$.

   Factoring: $3x^2 + x - 2 = (x + 1)(3x - 2) = 0$; $x = -1$ or $\frac{2}{3}$.

   There are two possible solutions, -1 and $\frac{2}{3}$. But it's necessary to be careful at this point and not assume that both are valid solutions of the given equation. Plugging the solution $x = -1$ back in the original equation we find that it reduces the denominators of both sides to zero. This is unacceptable. Therefore, $x = -1$ is an invalid or "extraneous" solution. Plugging the value $x = \frac{2}{3}$ back into the equation, we find that both sides turn out to be equal. Hence, this is a valid solution.

(Rigorous) (Skill 7.7)

32. Sam and Max are brothers. The difference in their heights is not more than 1.5 feet. If Max's height is 4.5 feet, what is Sam's height x in feet?

   A. $x = 6$
   B. $x = 3$
   C. $3 < x < 6$
   D. $x > 6$

   Answer: C. $3 < x < 6$

   Sam's height is given by the solution of the absolute value equation $|x - 4.5| < 1.5$, i.e., $(x - 4.5) < 1.5$ and $-(x - 4.5) > 1.5$; $x < 6$ and $x > 3$. This can be written as $3 < x < 6$.

(Rigorous) (Skill 8.1)

33. The graph shown below represents the following function:

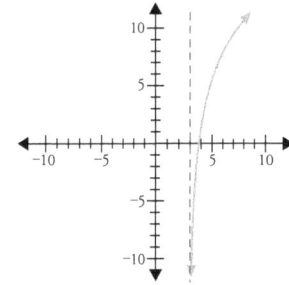

   A. $\ln x + 3$
   B. $\ln x - 3$
   C. $5 \ln(x - 3) + 3$
   D. $\ln(x + 3) + 5$

Answer: C. $5 \ln(x - 3) + 3$

The graph shows a vertical asymptote at $x = 3$, i.e., when $x - 3 = 0$. For a logarithmic function, this occurs when the argument of the logarithm is zero. Therefore the function must include the term $\ln(x - 3)$.

(Rigorous) (Skill 8.2)

34. The function $y = ab^{-x} + c$, where a, b, and c are constants, has:

    A. A y-intercept at $y = a + c$ and a horizontal asymptote at $y = c$

    B. A y-intercept at $y = c$ and no horizontal asymptote

    C. A y-intercept at $y = a + c$ and no horizontal asymptote

    D. A y-intercept at $y = a + c$ and a horizontal asymptote at $y = a$

Answer: A. A y-intercept at $y = a + c$ and a horizontal asymptote at $y = c$

The y-intercept of a function is the value of the function for $x = 0$. When $x = 0$, the function shown has the value $a + c$. For large values of x, the first term of the function goes to zero and the function goes asymptotically to c.

(Rigorous) (Skill 8.3)

35. If $\log_a x = c$ and $\log_b x = d$, then $\log_b a$ is equal to:

    A. $\frac{c}{d}$
    B. $\frac{d}{c}$
    C. cd
    D. None of the above

Answer: B. $\frac{d}{c}$

$\log_a x = c \Rightarrow x = a^c$ and $\log_b x = d \Rightarrow x = b^d$. Setting these equal to each other, $a^c = b^d \Rightarrow a = b^{\frac{d}{c}} \Rightarrow \log_b a = \frac{d}{c}$.

This can also be determined using the change of base formula, $\log_a x = \frac{\log_b x}{\log_b a}$.

(Rigorous) (Skill 8.4)

36. Solve $e^{2x} - 3e^x + 2 = 0$.

    A. $x = 1, 2$
    B. $x = \ln 2$
    C. $x = 0$
    D. $x = \ln 2, 0$

Answer: D. $x = \ln 2, 0$

Note that the equation $e^{2x} - 3e^x + 2 = 0$ is in the form of a quadratic equation since it can be written as $(e^x)^2 - 3e^x + 2 = 0$. Substituting $e^x = p$, we can solve the equation $p^2 - 3p + 2$ for p by factoring: $p^2 - 3p + 2 = 0; (p - 2)(p - 1) = 0; p = 2$ or $p = 1$.

Thus we have $e^x = 2$ or $e^x = 1$. Taking the natural logarithm of both sides: $x = \ln 2$ or $x = 0$.

(Rigorous) (Skill 8.8)

37. A lump of dough has been placed in a warm oven to rise. For several hours the volume of the dough increases by 50% every half hour. If the initial volume of the dough is V_0, the volume V after t hours is given by:

    A. $V = V_0(1.5)^{2t}$
    B. $V = V_0(0.5)^{2t}$
    C. $V = V_0(1.5)^t$
    D. $V = V_0(0.5)^t$

Answer: A. $V = V_0(1.5)^{2t}$

Since the volume increases by 50% every half hour, after the first half hour, the volume is 1.5 times the original volume. For every half hour after that it increases by a factor of 1.5. Since there are $2t$ half hours in t hours, the volume after t hours is $V = V_0(1.5)^{2t}$.

(Easy) (Skill 9.1)

38. **The sine function corresponding to a point on the unit circle has a positive value in quadrants:**

    A. I and II
    B. I and III
    C. I and IV
    D. II and IV

Answer: A. I and II

The mnemonic for remembering this is "all, sin, tan, cos," i.e., all three functions sine, tangent, and cosine are positive in quadrant I and only sine is positive in quadrant II.

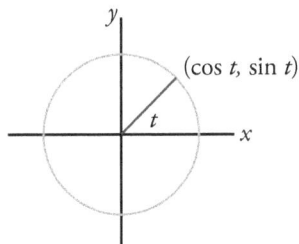

Another way to think of this is that a point on the unit circle can be written as $(\cos t, \sin t)$ where t is the angle formed by the radius of the circle to that point with the positive x-axis, i.e., $\sin t$ corresponds to the y-coordinate of the point. Hence, it is positive wherever the y-coordinate is positive, i.e., above the x-axis.

(Rigorous) (Skill 9.3)

39. **The graph shown below represents the function:**

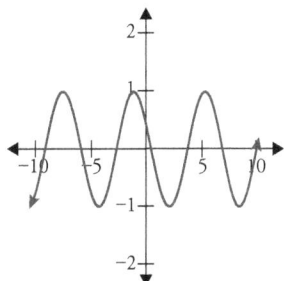

A. $\cos(x)$
B. $\cos\left(\frac{\pi}{3}x\right)$
C. $\cos\left(\frac{\pi}{3} + x\right)$
D. $\cos\left(\frac{\pi}{3} - x\right)$

Answer: C. $\cos\left(\frac{\pi}{3} + x\right)$

Since $\cos(0) = 1$, the peak values of the functions $\cos(x)$ and $\cos\left(\frac{\pi}{3}x\right)$ would both be at $x = 0$, which is not the case in this graph. For $\cos\left(\frac{\pi}{3} + x\right)$, the peak value is at $\frac{\pi}{3} + x = 0 \Rightarrow x = -\frac{\pi}{3} = -1.05$. For $\cos\left(\frac{\pi}{3} - x\right)$, the peak value is at $\frac{\pi}{3} - x = 0 \Rightarrow x = \frac{\pi}{3} = 1.05$. From the graph we see that C is the correct choice.

(Average) (Skill 9.4)

40. **A ramp is used to load boxes onto a truck. If the bed of the truck is 4 feet above the ground and the ramp is 6 feet long, what angle does the ramp make with the ground?**

    A. 42°
    B. 48°
    C. 34°
    D. 60°

Answer: A. 42°

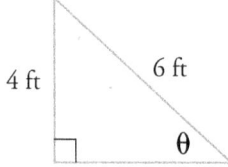

The sine of the angle θ that the ramp makes with the ground is given by $\sin \theta = \frac{4}{6} = \frac{2}{3}$.

Taking the inverse of this sine value, we get $\theta = \sin^{-1}\left(\frac{2}{3}\right) = 42°$.

(Rigorous) (Skill 9.5)

41. **Solve $\tan x + \cot x = 4$.**

    A. 60°

    B. 45°

    C. 30°

    D. 15°

Answer: D. 15°

$\tan x + \cot x = 4 \Rightarrow \frac{\sin x}{\cos x} + \frac{\cos x}{\sin x} = 4 \Rightarrow \frac{\sin^2 x + \cos^2 x}{\sin x \cos x} = 4$

Using the Pythagorean identity $\sin^2 x + \cos^2 x = 1$ and the double angle identity $\sin(2x) = 2 \sin x \cos x$, we get
$\frac{1}{\frac{1}{2}\sin(2x)} = 4 \Rightarrow 1 = 2 \sin(2x) \Rightarrow$
$\sin(2x) = \frac{1}{2} \Rightarrow 2x = 30° \Rightarrow x = 15°$.

(Rigorous) (Skill 9.6)

42. **The motion of a pendulum is modeled by the function $5 \sin\left(\frac{\pi t}{3}\right)$ where t is the time in seconds. What is the period of the pendulum's swing?**

    A. 3 seconds

    B. 5 seconds

    C. 6 seconds

    D. 15 seconds

Answer: C. 6 seconds

The function $y = \sin x$ has a period of 2π, i.e., it goes through a complete cycle within that span of x. The function $y = 5 \sin\left(\frac{\pi t}{3}\right)$ goes through a complete cycle in the time given by

$\frac{\pi t}{3} = 2\pi \Rightarrow \frac{t}{3} = 2 \Rightarrow t = 6$.

(Average) (Skill 10.1)

43. **A function $f(x)$ is continuous at $x = a$ if:**

    I. $f(a)$ is defined

    II. $\lim_{x \to a} f(x)$ exists

    III. $\lim_{x \to a} f(x) = f(a)$

    A. I only

    B. I and II

    C. I, II, and III

    D. None of the above

Answer: C. I, II, and III

By the definition of continuity, all three conditions given above have to be satisfied for a function $f(x)$ to be continuous at $x = a$.

ANSWERS WITH RATIONALES

(Average) (Skill 10.1)

44. In the graph shown below, the average rate of change of the function between points *A* and *B* is given by:

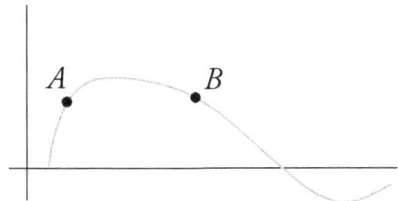

A. The slope of the tangent at point *A*
B. The slope of the tangent at point *B*
C. The slope of the line joining *A* and *B*
D. None of the above

Answer: C. The slope of the line joining *A* and *B*

The slope of the tangent at any point gives the instantaneous rate of change of the function at that point. The average rate of change of the function between two points is given by the slope of the secant line joining the two points.

(Average) (Skill 10.3)

45. In the graph of the function $f(x)$ shown below, at point *A*:

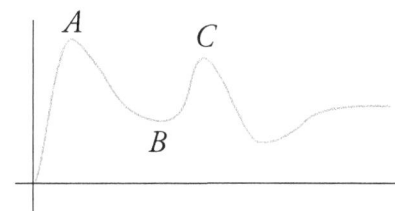

A. $f'(x) = 0$ and $f''(x) = 0$
B. $f'(x) = 0$ and $f''(x) > 0$
C. $f'(x) = 0$ and $f''(x) < 0$
D. $f'(x) < 0$ and $f''(x) < 0$

Answer: C. $f'(x) = 0$ and $f''(x) < 0$

The relative maxima and minima of a function correspond to $f'(x) = 0$. The relative maxima correspond to points where $f''(x) < 0$ and the relative minima correspond to points where $f''(x) > 0$. Since the point *A* is a relative maximum, $f'(x) = 0$ and $f''(x) < 0$.

(Rigorous) (Skill 10.4)

46. The function $\frac{x^3}{3} + \frac{x^2}{2} + x$ is the indefinite integral of the function:

A. $x^2 + x + 1$
B. $\frac{x^4}{12} + \frac{x^3}{6} + \frac{x^2}{2}$
C. $\frac{x^2}{2} + x$
D. $\frac{x^3}{3} + \frac{x^2}{2}$

Answer: A. $x^2 + x + 1$

According to the Fundamental Theorem of Calculus, $\frac{x^3}{3} + \frac{x^2}{2} + x$ is the indefinite integral of the function that is its derivative. The derivative of $\frac{x^3}{3} + \frac{x^2}{2} + x$ is $x^2 + x + 1$.

(Rigorous) (Skill 10.5)

47. The work done by a force $F(x)$ applied on an object from position $x = 0$ to $x = a$ is given by the integral $\int_0^a F(x)dx$. If $F(x) = mx + n$, where m and n are constants, what is the work done when the force $F(x)$ is applied from $x = 0$ to $x = a$?

   A. $ma + n$
   B. $\frac{1}{2}ma^2$
   C. $\frac{1}{2}ma^2 + na$
   D. $\frac{1}{2}ma^2 + n$

Answer: C. $\frac{1}{2}ma^2 + na$

Work done by the force =
$\int_0^a F(x)dx = \int_0^a (mx + n)dx = \left(\frac{1}{2}mx^2 + nx\right)\Big|_0^a$
$= \frac{1}{2}ma^2 + na$

(Average) (Skill 11.1)

48. Acceleration is the rate of change of speed, which has the units m/s (meters/second). What is the unit for the rate of change of acceleration?

   A. m/s^2
   B. m/s^3
   C. m^2/s
   D. m^2/s^2

Answer: B. m/s^3

The unit for acceleration is $(m/s)/s = m/s^2$. The unit for the rate of change of acceleration is $(m/s^2)/s = m/s^3$.

(Average) (Skill 11.2)

49. A cylinder and a cone both have the same radius and the same height. What is the ratio of the volume of the cylinder to the volume of the cone?

   A. 3
   B. $\frac{1}{3}$
   C. $\frac{1}{2}$
   D. 4

Answer: A. 3

The volume of a cylinder of radius r and height $h = \pi r^2 h$.

The volume of a cone of radius r and height $h = \frac{1}{3}\pi r^2 h$.

The ratio of the volume of the cylinder to the volume of the cone $= \frac{\pi r^2 h}{\frac{1}{3}\pi r^2 h} = 3$.

(Easy) (Skill 11.3)

50. The side of a cube is increased by a factor of 1.5. Its volume is increased by a factor of:

   A. 1.5
   B. 2.25
   C. 3.375
   D. 4.525

Answer: C. 3.375

A cube of side a has a volume of a^3. A cube of side $1.5a$ has a volume of $(1.5a)^3 = 3.375a^3$. Hence the volume of the cube increases by a factor of 3.375.

ANSWERS WITH RATIONALES

(Easy) (Skill 11.4)

51. **A 30°-60°-90° triangle has a hypotenuse 15 cm long. What is the length of its shortest side?**

    A. 7.5 cm

    B. 5 cm

    C. 8.66 cm

    D. 1.73 cm

Answer: A. 7.5 cm

In a 30°-60°-90° triangle, the length of the hypotenuse is double that of the shortest side. Therefore, the shortest side of the given triangle is 15 ÷ 2 = 7.5 cm.

(Rigorous) (Skill 11.6)

52. **Find the area enclosed by the parabola $f(x) = x^2$ and the line $y = 4$.**

    A. $\frac{8}{3}$

    B. $\frac{10}{3}$

    C. $\frac{20}{3}$

    D. 5

Answer: C. $\frac{20}{3}$

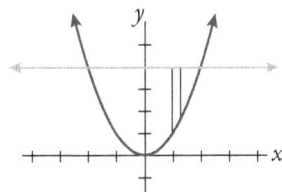

The parabola and line intersect at the points (-2, 4) and (2, 4). The area enclosed can be found by subdividing the area into thin vertical strips like the one shown and integrating between these bounds.

The length of a strip of thickness dx at a distance x from the y-axis = $3 - x^2$.

The area of the strip = $(3 - x^2)dx$.

Integrating from $x = -2$ to $x = 2$, we get

$$\int_{-2}^{2}(3 - x^2)dx = \left(3x - \frac{x^3}{3}\right)\Big|_{-2}^{2}$$
$$= \left(6 - \frac{8}{3}\right) - \left(-6 + \frac{8}{3}\right) = 12 - \frac{16}{3} = \frac{20}{3}.$$

(Easy) (Skill 12.2)

53. **What is the minimum number of noncollinear points needed to define a plane?**

    A. 1

    B. 2

    C. 3

    D. 4

Answer: C. 3

Given three noncollinear points, there is only one plane that can contain all three. Therefore, three points are sufficient to uniquely define a plane.

(Easy) (Skill 12.3)

54. **Triangles bounded by parallel lines, as shown below, have the same:**

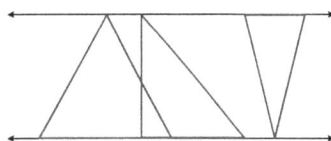

    A. Base

    B. Height

    C. Area

    D. Angles

Answer: B. Height

Since parallel lines are separated by the same distance at all points, each of these triangles has the same height.

(Average) (Skill 12.4)

55. In the diagram shown below, $AB \cong BC$ and DB bisects $\angle ABC$. The triangles DAB and DCB can be proven to be congruent using:

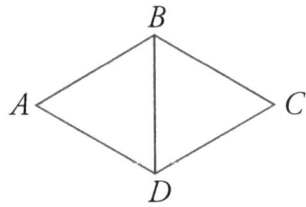

A. SSS

B. SAS

C. AAS

D. HL

Answer: B. SAS

It is given that $AB \cong BC$. Since DB bisects $\angle ABC$, $\angle ABD \cong \angle CBD$. $BD \cong BD$ through the reflexive property. Therefore the two triangles can be proven congruent using SAS.

(Average) (Skill 12.5)

56. The purpose of the construction shown below is to:

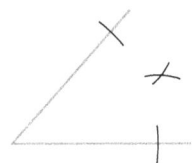

A. Draw a perpendicular line to one of the sides

B. Bisect the angle

C. Trisect the angle

D. Draw a right triangle

Answer: B. Bisect the angle

A line joining the vertex of the angle to the intersecting arcs will bisect the angle.

(Average) (Skill 12.7)

57. Euclid's fifth axiom, the parallel postulate:

   I. Can be proven using the other axioms

   II. Does not hold for non-Euclidean geometries

A. Only I is true

B. Only II is true

C. Both I and II are true

D. Neither I nor II is true

Answer: B. Only II is true

Many mathematicians over the ages thought that the parallel postulate was not needed because it could be proven using the other axioms. This assumption turned out to be wrong because it was possible to conceive of other (non-Euclidean) geometries where the parallel postulate is not valid.

(Average) (Skill 13.1)

58. A regular polygon with each interior angle equal to 108 degrees is a(n):

A. Pentagon

B. Hexagon

C. Heptagon

D. Octagon

Answer: A. Pentagon

Each interior angle of a regular polygon with n sides has a measure of $\frac{180(n-2)}{n}$ degrees. Here $\frac{180(n-2)}{n} = 108$
$\Rightarrow 180(n-2) = 108n$
$\Rightarrow 180n - 360 = 108n \Rightarrow 72n = 360$
$\Rightarrow n = \frac{360}{72} = 5$.

ANSWERS WITH RATIONALES

(Average) (Skill 13.2)

59. **When two chords intersect inside a circle and each chord is divided into two smaller segments:**

   A. The sum of the lengths of the two segments formed from one chord equals the sum of the lengths of the two segments formed from the other chord

   B. The chords bisect each other

   C. The chords are perpendicular to each other

   D. The product of the lengths of the two segments formed from one chord equals the product of the lengths of the two segments formed from the other chord

Answer: D. The product of the lengths of the two segments formed from one chord equals the product of the lengths of the two segments formed from the other chord

If two chords intersect inside a circle, each chord is divided into two smaller segments. The product of the lengths of the two segments formed from one chord equals the product of the lengths of the two segments formed from the other chord.

(Rigorous) (Skill 13.3)

60. **Which of the following three-dimensional figures does not belong with the others?**

   cone, cylinder, rectangular prism, triangular prism

   A. Cone

   B. Cylinder

   C. Rectangular prism

   D. Triangular prism

Answer: A. Cone

A cylinder is essentially a prism since it has two identical parallel bases. As for all prisms, the volume of a cylinder is given by the product of the area of its base and its height.

(Average) (Skill 13.4)

61. **The perimeter of the composite figure shown is:**

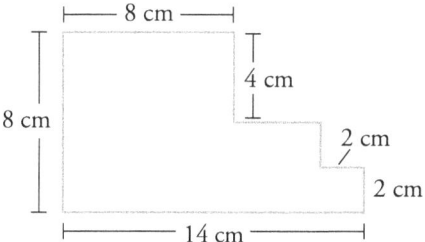

   A. 28 cm

   B. 32 cm

   C. 38 cm

   D. 44 cm

Answer: D. 44 cm

Adding up all the sides of the figure, we get $8 + 8 + 4 + 4 + 2 + 2 + 2 + 14 = 44$ cm.

(Rigorous) (Skill 13.5)

62. **Which of the following cross-sections can be obtained by cutting through a right circular cylinder?**

   I. Circle

   II. Ellipse

   III. Rectangle

   A. I only

   B. I and II

   C. I and III

   D. I, II, and III

Answer: D. I, II, and III

A cut parallel to the bases of a cylinder will produce a circle while a cut perpendicular to the bases will result in a rectangle. A slant cut through a cylinder will produce an ellipse.

(Easy) (Skill 13.7)

63. **A 20-foot by 18-foot room is to be covered with hardwood flooring. The flooring material comes in planks of different sizes. Which of the following available sizes may be used to cover the area with minimum wastage?**

    A. 3 ft. by 5 ft.

    B. 3 ft. by 7 ft.

    C. 4 ft. by 4 ft.

    D. 4 ft. by 8 ft.

Answer: A. 3 ft. by 5 ft.

Since 3 is a factor of 18 and 5 is a factor of 20, the floor can be covered completely with 3 ft. by 5 ft. planks without discarding any of the material. All of the other choices will require some of the planks to be cut and some of the material to be discarded.

(Average) (Skill 14.1)

64. **Which of the following geometric transformations retains both the original size and original orientation of an object?**

    A. Reflection

    B. Rotation

    C. Translation

    D. Dilation

Answer: C. Translation

Reflection and rotation do not change the size of an object although the orientation is changed. Dilation changes the size, not the orientation. Only translation, a "sliding transformation," leaves both size and orientation unchanged.

(Average) (Skill 14.3)

65. **A rectangle is symmetric under which of the following rotations in the plane?**

    I. 90°

    II. 180°

    III. 360°

    A. I

    B. I and II

    C. II and III

    D. I, II, and III

Answer: C. II and III

A rectangle remains unchanged in orientation when it is rotated 180° or 360° in the plane.

(Rigorous) (Skill 14.4)

66. **A square with corners at (−3, 3), (3, 3), (3, −3), and (−3, −3) on the coordinate plane is dilated with a scale factor of 2 and the center of dilation at the origin. The corners of the transformed square are at:**

    A. (−6, 6), (6, 6), (3, −3), and (−3, −3)

    B. (−3, 3), (3, 3), (6, −6), and (−6, −6)

    C. (−3, 3), (3, 3), (9, −9), and (−9, −9)

    D. (−6, 6), (6, 6), (6, −6), and (−6, −6)

Answer: D. (−6, 6), (6, 6), (6, −6), and (−6, −6)

Since the origin is the center of dilation, the center of the square remains at the origin. Since the scale factor is 2, all the dimensions of the square are doubled. Therefore all the coordinates of the corners are doubled.

(Rigorous) (Skill 14.5)

67. A quadrilateral has corners at (-3, 3), (3, 3), (0, -3), and (6, -3) on the coordinate plane. Which of the following is true?

    I. The quadrilateral is a parallelogram
    II. The diagonals of the quadrilateral are perpendicular to each other

    A. I only
    B. II only
    C. I and II
    D. Neither I nor II

Answer: A. I only

The side joining points (-3, -3) and (3, 3) is parallel to the x-axis. So is the side joining points (0, -3) and (6, -3). Both of these are 6 units in length. Since these opposite sides are parallel and equal in length, the figure is a parallelogram.

The slope of the diagonal joining points (-3, 3) and (6, -3) = $\frac{(-3-3)}{(6+3)} = \frac{-6}{9} = -\frac{2}{3}$.

The slope of the diagonals joining points (3, 3) and (0, -3) = $\frac{(-3-3)}{(0-3)} = \frac{(-6)}{(-3)} = 2$.

The diagonals are not perpendicular since their product is not equal to -1.

(Rigorous) (Skill 14.6)

68. The equation $ax^2 + by^2 = c^2$, where a, b, and c are constants, is the equation of a circle if:

    A. $a = b, c > 0$
    B. $a = b, a > 0, b > 0$
    C. $a = b = c$
    D. $a = b, a < 0, b < 0$

Answer: B. $a = b, a > 0, b > 0$

The general equation of a circle is $x^2 + y^2 = r^2$. The equation $ax^2 + by^2 = c^2$ can be cast in this form only when $a = b, a > 0, b > 0$.

(Rigorous) (Skill 14.8)

69. Vectors $ai + bj$ and $ci + dj$ (where a, b, c, d are constants) are perpendicular to each other when:

    A. $ab = cd$
    B. $ac = bd$
    C. $ac + bd = 0$
    D. $ad + bc = 0$

Answer: C. $ac + bd = 0$

Two vectors are perpendicular to each other when their dot product is zero. The dot product of $ai + bj$ and $ci + dj$ is $ac + bd$.

(Average) (Skill 15.1)

70. A survey is conducted to collect data about preferred ice cream flavors. People are asked to rank five flavors in order of preference. The kind of measurement scale used is:

    A. Nominal
    B. Ordinal
    C. Interval
    D. Ratio

    Answer: B. Ordinal

    The data gathered is the order of preference, which is measured using an ordinal scale. If respondents were asked to pick just their favorite flavor, the scale used would be a nominal one. Since quantitative measurements are not made, the scale used is not interval or ratio form.

(Easy) (Skill 15.1)

71. In a box-and-whisker plot, the box is drawn from:

    A. The first quartile to the median
    B. The median to the third quartile
    C. The first quartile to the third quartile
    D. None of the above

    Answer: C. The first quartile to the third quartile

    The box shows the middle half of the data, i.e., it is drawn from the 25th percentile (first quartile) point to the 75th percentile (third quartile) point.

(Average) (Skill 15.3)

72. The data distribution shown below is:

    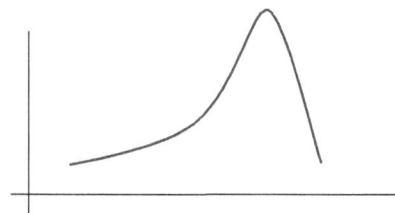

    A. Symmetric
    B. Skewed to the left
    C. Skewed to the right
    D. Bimodal

    Answer: B. Skewed to the left

    Because the distribution has a longer "tail" toward the left, it is said to be skewed to the left.

(Rigorous) (Skill 15.4)

73. In the data distribution shown in question 72:

    A. The mean and mode are both at the peak
    B. The mean is to the left of the mode
    C. The mean is to the right of the mode
    D. Both the mean and median are to the left of the peak

    Answer: B. The mean is to the left of the mode

    The mode is at the peak of the distribution since that is where the highest frequency of data points exists. The drawn-out tail toward the left results in an average or mean that is located to the left of the peak.

(Rigorous) (Skill 15.5)

74. The following linear transformation indicates a simple translation of the data without any stretching or shrinking:

    A. $X' = X + 3$
    B. $X' = 2X + 3$
    C. $X' = 5X + 1$
    D. $X' = 3X$

    Answer: A. $X' = X + 3$

    In a linear transformation, the additive component represents a translation while the multiplicative component represents a stretching or shrinking. Option A is the only answer choice in which X is not multiplied by a factor.

(Rigorous) (Skill 15.6)

75. The measure of central tendency most affected by including an outlier in a data set is the:

    A. Median
    B. Mean
    C. Mode
    D. Mean and mode

    Answer: B. Mean

    The mean is affected most since it measures the average value of the data points in the set, and the value of an outlier is far outside the range of the other data points. The median and mode are less affected since they depend on the location of a data point in a set, not its value.

(Rigorous) (Skill 16.1)

76. A coin tossing experiment yields five heads in a row. This indicates that:

    A. There is a lower chance of getting a head in the next toss
    B. The coin is weighted
    C. The experimental procedure is flawed
    D. None of the above

    Answer: D. None of the above

    Each coin toss is independent. So the chance of getting a head is always $\frac{1}{2}$ and does not depend on what happened earlier. The fact that the probability of a coin toss yielding a head is $\frac{1}{2}$ only indicates that over a large number of tosses about half the tosses will result in heads; it says nothing about the pattern of successive heads and tails.

(Easy) (Skill 16.2)

77. Melanie, Maria, Ethel, Elizabeth, Rita, Gilda, and Renee put their names in a hat and draw one name to decide who will pay for everybody's lunch. What is the probability that a name without an "e" in it will be drawn?

    A. $\frac{3}{7}$
    B. $\frac{4}{7}$
    C. $\frac{2}{7}$
    D. $\frac{5}{7}$

    Answer: A. $\frac{3}{7}$

    Out of the 7 names, Maria, Rita, and Gilda are the 3 names that do not have any "e"s in them. Therefore the probability of drawing a name without an "e" in it is $\frac{3}{7}$.

(Rigorous) (Skill 16.4)

78. A drawer has 3 blue socks, 8 red socks, and 5 green socks in it. If 3 socks are pulled out of the drawer at random, what is the probability that all 3 are blue?

   A. $\frac{3}{16}$

   B. $\frac{1}{560}$

   C. $\frac{1}{1120}$

   D. $\frac{1}{1680}$

Answer: B. $\frac{1}{560}$

The number of ways 3 socks can be drawn from a total of $16 = {}^{16}C_3 = \frac{16!}{3!13!} = \frac{14 \cdot 15 \cdot 16}{2 \cdot 3} = 560$.

There is only one way 3 blue socks can be drawn from the set of 16.

Therefore, the probability of all 3 socks being blue $= \frac{1}{560}$.

Another way to think about this problem:

The probability of the first sock being blue $= \frac{3}{16}$.

After the first blue sock is taken out, there are 2 blue socks and a total of 15 socks remaining in the drawer. So the probability of the second sock also being blue $= \frac{2}{15}$.

Similarly, the probability of the third sock being blue $= \frac{1}{14}$.

Therefore, the probability of all 3 socks being blue $= \left(\frac{3}{16}\right)\left(\frac{2}{15}\right)\left(\frac{1}{14}\right) = \frac{1}{560}$.

(Rigorous) (Skill 16.5)

79. A dart board has a square in the center of a circle. If the side of the square is 7 inches and the probability of a dart hitting the square is 0.3, what is the radius of the circle in inches?

   A. 7.2

   B. 2.1

   C. 23.3

   D. 14.0

Answer: A. 7.2

Let the radius of the circle be r. Since the probability of a dart hitting the square is equal to the ratio of the areas of the square and circle,

$\frac{49}{\pi r^2} = 0.3$; $r^2 = \frac{49}{0.3\pi} = 52$; $r = 7.2$ inches.

(Average) (Skill 16.6)

80. In a high school class of 30 children, 10 take French, 12 take Spanish, and 3 take both French and Spanish. What is the probability that a student chosen at random from the class takes French or Spanish?

   A. $\frac{11}{15}$

   B. $\frac{2}{15}$

   C. $\frac{19}{30}$

   D. $\frac{25}{30}$

Answer: C. $\frac{19}{30}$

According to the addition rule for two events A and B that are not mutually exclusive, $P(A \text{ or } B) = P(A) + P(B) - P(A \text{ and } B)$ where $P(A)$ is defined as the probability of event A.

The probability of a student taking French $= \frac{10}{30}$.

The probability of a student taking Spanish $= \frac{12}{30}$.

The probability of a student taking both French and Spanish $= \frac{3}{30}$.

Therefore, the probability of a student taking French or Spanish $= \frac{10}{30} + \frac{12}{30} - \frac{3}{30} = \frac{19}{30}$.

(Rigorous) (Skill 16.7)

81. **The expected value of a random variable is:**

    A. The mean value that would be obtained from an infinite number of observations
    B. The average of possible values weighted by the probability of each
    C. The integral of a continuous random variable multiplied by its probability density function over its range of values
    D. All of the above

Answer: D. All of the above

All of the given options are correct. Expected value is a generalization of the concept of mean or average taking into account the probability of each event or observation.

(Easy) (Skill 17.1)

82. **To study how effective a drug is in treating a disease, the best method of data collection is a(n):**

    A. Census
    B. Sample survey
    C. Controlled experiment
    D. Observational study

Answer: C. Controlled experiment

A controlled experiment is the best way to investigate a cause-and-effect relationship since the experimenter can ensure the random assignment of subjects to groups and treatments to subjects.

(Average) (Skill 17.2)

83. **Most of the employees in a company earn less than $100,000. The CEO earns $1,000,000. An article about the company states that the average salary is $110,000. Which of the following statements are correct?**

    I. The information in the article is not misleading since $110,000 is the actual average amount earned by company employees.
    II. The information in the article is misleading since an outlier has been included in calculating the average.
    III. Instead of the mean, a different measure of central tendency such as the median should have been selected.

    A. I and II
    B. I and III
    C. II and III
    D. I, II, and III

Answer: C. II and III

The information in the article is accurate but misleading since it gives readers the wrong impression about how much the company employees earn. In this case, the median would be a much better measure of central tendency.

POSTTEST

(Average) (Skill 17.3)

84. **In a survey, the sample is chosen such that all racial groups are represented.**

    What is this method of sampling called?

    A. Random

    B. Systematic

    C. Stratified

    D. Cluster

    Answer: C. Stratified

    In stratified sampling, the population is divided into groups based on some chosen characteristic, such as race. A sample is then chosen from each of these groups using one of the other methods of sampling. This is the sampling method described here.

(Rigorous) (Skill 17.4)

85. **What is the probability of getting 7 heads in a series of 10 coin flips?**

    A. 0.12

    B. 0.5

    C. 0.7

    D. 0.9

    Answer: A. 0.12

    A binomial distribution deals with situations in which there are two outcomes, success and failure. The probability of k successes in n trials is given by $^nC_k \cdot p^k \cdot (1-p)^{n-k}$ where p is the probability of success in a single trial.

    In the given problem, $n = 10$, $k = 7$, and $p = 0.5$, where success is defined as getting a head.

    So the probability of getting 7 heads in 10 tosses = $^{10}C_7 \cdot (0.5)^7 \cdot (0.5)^3 = \frac{10!}{7!3!} \cdot (0.5)^7 \cdot (0.5)^3 = 120 \cdot (0.5)^7 \cdot (0.5)^3 = 0.12$.

(Average) (Skill 17.5)

86. **Given the following set of (x, y) points, which regression line best fits the data?**

    $(0, 0)$, $(1, 0.6)$, $(2, 1.25)$, $(3, 2.1)$, $(4, 2.5)$

    A. $y = \frac{1}{20}x$

    B. $y = -\frac{1}{20}x$

    C. $y = \frac{2}{3}x$

    D. $y = -\frac{2}{3}x$

    Answer: C. $y = \frac{2}{3}x$

    Since y increases as x increases, the line must have a positive slope. So Options B and D are incorrect. Inspection of the data shows that it fits much closer to $y = \frac{2}{3}x$ than to $y = \frac{1}{20}x$.

(Rigorous) (Skill 17.6)

87. **In order to fit to the exponential regression function $y = ae^{bx}$, nonlinear data can be transformed to linear form by:**

    A. Taking the reciprocal

    B. Taking the natural logarithm

    C. Taking the square root

    D. Squaring

    Answer: B. Taking the natural logarithm

    Taking the natural logarithm of the data will allow the transformed data to be fitted to a linear equation as follows:

    $\ln y = \ln(ae^{bx}) = \ln a + \ln e^{bx} = \ln a + bx$.

The values of a and b obtained can then be used to fit the original data set to the exponential function $y = ae^{bx}$.

(Average) (Skill 18.1)
88. **In a mathematical proof, a premise is:**
    A. A given statement that is true
    B. A given statement that is assumed to be true
    C. A given statement that is false but is assumed to be true
    D. Reasoning provided to support a statement

Answer: B. A given statement that is assumed to be true

A premise is an initial statement that is assumed to be true. All subsequent reasoning is carried out on the basis of that assumption. The premise may or may not actually be true.

(Average) (Skill 18.2)
89. **The conclusion "Alex is a swimmer" can be drawn from the following premises:**
    A. All boys from East high school are swimmers. Alex is a student at East high school.
    B. One of the students at East high school is a swimmer. Alex is one of the students at East high school.
    C. All students from East high school are swimmers. Alex is a student at East high school.
    D. All of the above

Answer: C. All students from East high school are swimmers. Alex is a student at East high school.

Option A is not valid since Alex may not be a boy. Option B is not valid since one of the students other than Alex might be the swimmer. Only the premises in Option C lead directly to the conclusion that Alex is a swimmer.

(Rigorous) (Skill 18.3)
90. **Matilda has left her home with an umbrella every morning for a week. One can use inductive reasoning to conjecture that:**
    I. Matilda will leave home with an umbrella the next morning
    II. It has been raining every morning for a week
    A. I only
    B. II only
    C. I and II
    D. Neither I nor II

Answer: A. I only

One can use inductive reasoning to conjecture that the observed pattern will continue but nothing more than that.

(Easy) (Skill 18.5)
91. **Guess-and-check is:**
    A. A valid strategy for solving a math problem
    B. A strategy used to understand a problem which must be solved using a different method
    C. An invalid method of problem-solving since it does not show understanding of concepts
    D. An invalid method of problem-solving since it does not follow logical steps

Answer: A. A valid strategy for solving a math problem

Guess-and-check may not always be the best way to solve a math problem, but it is a perfectly valid problem-solving strategy. At the least it can be a good beginning strategy to improve understanding when it is not clear what other method can be used to solve a problem.

(Average) (Skill 19.1)

92. The points (0, 3) and (5, 3) can be used to represent:

    A. A horizontal line
    B. The side of a square
    C. The side of a triangle
    D. All of the above

Answer: D. All of the above

The two points can be used to represent the horizontal line $y = 3$ that passes through them, two corners of a square, or two vertices of a triangle.

(Easy) (Skill 19.3)

93. The equation $y = \frac{3}{x}$ can be expressed verbally as:

    I. y is equal to 3 divided by x
    II. y is equal to 3 times the reciprocal of x
    III. The product of x and y is equal to 3

    A. I only
    B. I and II
    C. I and III
    D. I, II, and III

Answer: D. I, II, and III

All of the three verbal expressions are equivalent to each other and to the given equation.

(Easy) (Skill 19.4)

94. This type of mathematical representation is typically not used in high school mathematics:

    A. Symbolic
    B. Pictorial
    C. Concrete
    D. Graphical

Answer: C. Concrete

A concrete representation of mathematical ideas involves manipulatives such as blocks or sticks. These are typically used with young children who have not yet developed the capacity for abstract thinking.

(Easy) (Skill 19.5)

95. A science project requires students to compare how rainfall patterns change from January to December for two consecutive years. The best way to analyze this information is to represent it:

    A. In table form
    B. As line graphs on the same coordinate axes with the lines drawn using different colors
    C. With separate pie charts for each year showing one month in each segment
    D. With bars of different colors on the same chart showing the rainfall for each month

Answer: B. As line graphs on the same coordinate axes with the lines drawn using different colors

Data trends can best be observed using line graphs. Putting them on the same chart will allow easy comparison between the two different sets of data for each of the two years.

(Average) (Skill 20.4)

96. **Stopwatches can be used in the mathematics classroom to enhance students' understanding of the concept of:**

    A. Measurement
    B. Intervals
    C. Precision
    D. Accuracy

Answer: C. Precision

Students learn about measurement, intervals, and accuracy right from elementary grades using many different tools such as rulers, protractors, and thermometers. They also learn about measurement of time using wristwatches and clocks. Stopwatches allow for more precise measurement of time in units smaller than a second. This gives students a better understanding of the concept of different degrees of precision.

(Average) (Skill 20.5)

97. **A teacher is introducing the concept of linear relationships to her class using equations, real-life examples, and tables and graphs. In what order should each of these instructional elements be introduced?**

    A. Equations, real-life examples, tables and graphs
    B. Real-life examples, tables and graphs, equations
    C. Real-life examples, equations, tables and graphs
    D. Equations, tables and graphs, real-life examples

Answer: B. Real-life examples, tables and graphs, equations

The sequence given in Option B represents a movement on the continuum from more concrete elements to more abstract ones. This is an effective and popular teaching strategy.

(Average) (Skill 20.8)

98. **Which of the following kinds of questioning strategies requires the highest level of thinking?**

    A. Synthesis of disparate information
    B. Test of knowledge
    C. Analysis of a concept into component parts
    D. Test of comprehension

Answer: A. Synthesis of disparate information

Test of knowledge is the simplest kind of questioning strategy, followed by comprehension, analysis, and synthesis. Each level requires the skills needed at each of the previous levels. In order to respond to a question that requires synthesis of information, a student must be able to recall information, understand it, and analyze it.

(Easy) (Skill 21.1)

99. **The purpose of a summative assessment is:**

    A. To assess whether a student is able to think outside the box

    B. To gather information so instruction can be improved

    C. To assess whether a student has met learning goals at the end of a unit

    D. To get an informal sense of how much a student knows

    Answer: C. To assess whether a student has met learning goals at the end of a unit

    The goal of summative assessment is to evaluate student learning at the end of an instructional unit.

(Average) (Skill 21.4)

100. **In order to use the results of assessments to improve instruction, a teacher must:**

    A. Assess prior knowledge of students

    B. Use frequent assessment strategies of different kinds

    C. Have a flexible instructional plan that can be modified

    D. All of the above

    Answer: D. All of the above

It is important to assess prior knowledge so that the teacher can evaluate the difference made by instruction. Frequent assessment of different kinds will provide the teacher with data to guide instruction. Finally, the instructional strategy must have room for change so that the teacher can use the results of assessment to modify teaching.

Answer: B. As line graphs on the same coordinate axes with the lines drawn using different colors

Data trends can best be observed using line graphs. Putting them on the same chart will allow easy comparison between the two different sets of data for each of the two years.

(Average) (Skill 20.4)

96. **Stopwatches can be used in the mathematics classroom to enhance students' understanding of the concept of:**

    A. Measurement
    B. Intervals
    C. Precision
    D. Accuracy

Answer: C. Precision

Students learn about measurement, intervals, and accuracy right from elementary grades using many different tools such as rulers, protractors, and thermometers. They also learn about measurement of time using wristwatches and clocks. Stopwatches allow for more precise measurement of time in units smaller than a second. This gives students a better understanding of the concept of different degrees of precision.

(Average) (Skill 20.5)

97. **A teacher is introducing the concept of linear relationships to her class using equations, real-life examples, and tables and graphs. In what order should each of these instructional elements be introduced?**

    A. Equations, real-life examples, tables and graphs
    B. Real-life examples, tables and graphs, equations
    C. Real-life examples, equations, tables and graphs
    D. Equations, tables and graphs, real-life examples

Answer: B. Real-life examples, tables and graphs, equations

The sequence given in Option B represents a movement on the continuum from more concrete elements to more abstract ones. This is an effective and popular teaching strategy.

(Average) (Skill 20.8)

98. **Which of the following kinds of questioning strategies requires the highest level of thinking?**

    A. Synthesis of disparate information
    B. Test of knowledge
    C. Analysis of a concept into component parts
    D. Test of comprehension

Answer: A. Synthesis of disparate information

Test of knowledge is the simplest kind of questioning strategy, followed by comprehension, analysis, and synthesis. Each level requires the skills needed at each of the previous levels. In order to respond to a question that requires synthesis of information, a student must be able to recall information, understand it, and analyze it.

(Easy) (Skill 21.1)

99. **The purpose of a summative assessment is:**

    A. To assess whether a student is able to think outside the box

    B. To gather information so instruction can be improved

    C. To assess whether a student has met learning goals at the end of a unit

    D. To get an informal sense of how much a student knows

    Answer: C. To assess whether a student has met learning goals at the end of a unit

    The goal of summative assessment is to evaluate student learning at the end of an instructional unit.

(Average) (Skill 21.4)

100. **In order to use the results of assessments to improve instruction, a teacher must:**

    A. Assess prior knowledge of students

    B. Use frequent assessment strategies of different kinds

    C. Have a flexible instructional plan that can be modified

    D. All of the above

    Answer: D. All of the above

It is important to assess prior knowledge so that the teacher can evaluate the difference made by instruction. Frequent assessment of different kinds will provide the teacher with data to guide instruction. Finally, the instructional strategy must have room for change so that the teacher can use the results of assessment to modify teaching.

More Study Tools to Help Pass Your Certification Exam

XAMonline.com

Pass your exam with our suite of superior study tools, including:

- Print books
- eBooks
- eFlashcards
- Web-based interactive study guides

Teaching in another state? XAMonline carries 500+ state-specific and PRAXIS study guides covering every test subject nationwide.

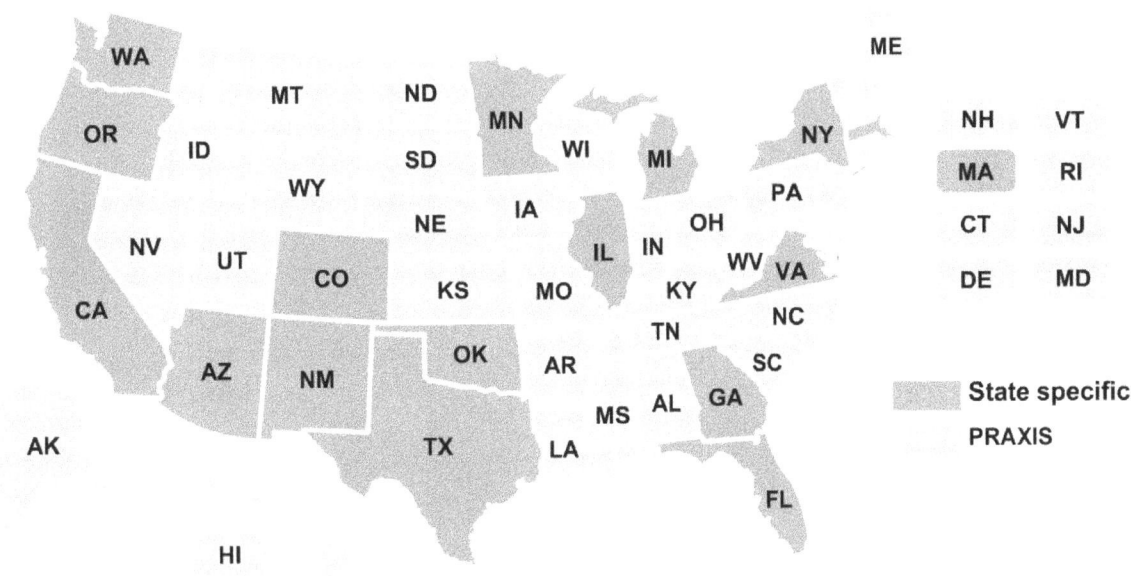

Call or visit us online!
800.301.4647 | www.XAMonline.com

www.ingramcontent.com/pod-product-compliance
Lightning Source LLC
Chambersburg PA
CBHW062132160426
43191CB00013B/2279